Lucifer's Rebellion

**A Tribute To
Christopher S. Hyatt, Ph.D.**

Some Other Titles From New Falcon Publications

Aha! The Sevenfold Mystery of the Ineffable Love	Aleister Crowley
An Insider's Guide to Robert Anton Wilson	Eric Wagner
Bio-Etheric Healing	Trudy Lanitis
Undoing Yourself With Energized Meditation and Other Devices, Secrets of Western Tantra: The Sexuality of the Middle Path, Dogma Daze	Christopher S. Hyatt, Ph.D.
Rebels & Devils; The Psychology of Liberation	Edited by Christopher S. Hyatt, Ph.D.
Aleister Crowley's Illustrated Goetia, Sex Magic, Tantra & Tarot: The Way of the Secret Lover, Taboo: Sex, Religion & Magick	C. S. Hyatt, Ph.D., and DuQuette
Pacts With The Devil, Urban Voodoo: A Beginner's Guide to Afro-Caribbean Magic	Jason Black and Christopher S. Hyatt, Ph.D.
The Psychopath's Bible	Christopher S. Hyatt, Ph.D., and Jack Willis
Ask Baba Lon	Lon Milo DuQuette
Aleister Crowley and the Treasure House of Images	J.F.C. Fuller, Aleister Crowley, Lon Milo DuQuette and Nancy Wasserman
Enochian Sex Magic and How To Workbook	Aleister Crowley, Lon Milo DuQuette and Christopher S. Hyatt, Ph.D.
Enochian World of Aleister Crowley	DuQuette and Aleister Crowley
Info-Psychology, Neuropolitique, The Game of Life, What Does WoMan Want?	Timothy Leary, Ph.D.
Paganism in Christian Holidays	J. M. Wheeler
Nonlocal Nature: The Eight Circuits of Consciousness	James A. Heffernan
Numbers Their Meaning and Magic, Vol I, and Vol II, Zodiacal Symbology and It's Planetary Power, Book One and Book Two	Isidore Kozminsky
on What is	Ja Wallin
Rebellion, Revolution and Religiousness	Osho
Reichian Therapy: A Practical Guide for Home Use	Dr. Jack Willis
Shaping Formless Fire, Seizing Power, Taking Power,	
The Magick in the Music and Other Essays	Stephen Mace
The Illuminati Conspiracy: The Sapiens System	Donald Holmes, M.D.
The Philosophy of Numbers, Vol I and Vol II, Nature's Symphony, Lessons in Number Vibration	Mrs. L. Dow Balliett
The Secret Inner Order Rituals of the Golden Dawn	Pat Zalewski
The Why, Who, and What of Existence	Vlad Korbel
Steamo Goes to Havana, The Social Epidemic of Child Abuse	Michael Miller, M.Ed., M.S., Ph.D.
Woman's Orgasm: A Guide to Sexual Satisfaction	Benjamin Graber, M.D., and Georgia Kline-Graber, R.N.
Zingara Art of Divinition	Ana Calaroni

Titles by J. Marvin Spiegelman, Ph.D.

A Modern Jew in Search of Soul
Buddhism and Jungian Psychology
Catholicism and Jungian Psychology
Hinduism and Jungian Psychology
Mysticism, Psychology and Oedipus - A Small Gem
Protestanism and Jungian Psychology
Psychotherapy and Religion at the Millennium and Beyond
Psychotherapy as a Mutual Process
Reich, Jung, Regardie & Me - The Unhealed Healer
Rider, Haggard, Henry Miller & I - The Unpublished Writer
Sufism, Islam and Jungian Psychology
The Knight - A Small Gem
The Nymphomaniac
The Quest - Further Adventures in the Unconscious
The Tree of Life - Paths in Jungian Individuation
The Wisdom of J. Marvin Speigelman Vol. I - Selected Writings
The Wisdom of J. Marvin Speigelman Vol. II - Psychology and Religion

Other Titles by Dr. Israel Regardie

A Garden of Pomegranates
A Practical Guide to Geomantic Divination - A Small Gem
Attract and Use Healing Energy - A Small Gem
Be Yourself - A Guide to Relaxation and Health
Ceremonial Magic
Dr. Israel Regardie's Definitive Work on Aleister Crowley, The Eye In The Triangle
Healing Energy, Prayer and Relaxation
How To Make and Use Talismans - A Small Gem
Israel Regardie's The Foundations of Practical Magick
My Rosicrucian Adventure
Mysticism, Psychology and Oedipus - A Small Gem
Practical Magick - A Small Gem
Teachers of Fulfillment
The Art and Meaning of Magic - A Small Gem
The Body-Mind Connection, A Path to Well-Being - A Small Gem
The Complete Golden Dawn System of Magic
The Complete Golden Dawn System of Magic Book 1 - Ltd. Edition
The Complete Golden Dawn System of Magic Book 2 - Ltd. Edition
The Complete Golden Dawn System of Magic - The Black Edition
The Eye in the Triangle: An Interpretation of Aleister Crowley
The Golden Dawn Audio CDs, Vol. 1, Vol. 2, and Vol. 3
The Legend of Aleister Crowley
The Magic of Israel Regardie
The Middle Pillar
The Philosopher's Stone
The Portable Complete Golden Dawn System of Magic
The Tree of Life
The Wisdom of Israel Regardie - Vol. I
  Selected Introductions, Prefaces and Forewords
The Wisdom of Israel Regardie - Vol. II
  Selected Essays and Commentaries
The Wisdom of Israel Regardie - Vol. III
  Selected Articles, Introductions, Prefaces and Forewords
What You Should Know About the Golden Dawn
Wilhelm Reich, His Theory And Techniques
Aha! (Dr. Israel Regardie and Aleister Crowley)
Roll Away The Stone/The Herb Dangerous
  (Dr. Israel Regardie and Aleister Crowley)

MANY OF OUR TITLES AVAILABLE ON KINDLE!
Please visit our website at http://www.newfalcon.com

Copyright ©New Falcon Publications 2024

All rights reserved. No part of this book, in part or in whole, may be reproduced, transmitted, or utilized, in any form or by any means, electronic or mechanical, including photocopying, recording, or by any information storage and retrieval system, without permission in writing from the publisher, except for brief quotations in critical articles, books and reviews.

ISBN 13: 978-1-56184-527-9

ISBN 10: 1-56184-527-2

First New Falcon Publications Edition 2024

The paper used in this publication meets the minimum requirements of the American National Standard for Permanence of Paper for Printed Library Materials Z39.48-1984

Printed in USA

NEW FALCON PUBLICATIONS
2046 Hillhurst Avenue
Los Angeles, CA 90027
www.newfalcon.com
email: info@newfalcon.com

Lucifer's Rebellion

A Tribute To
Christopher S. Hyatt, Ph.D.

Edited with a Foreword by Shelly Marmor
Preface by Lon Milo DuQuette
Introduction by Jeff Mandon

Timothy Leary, Ph.D. • Eric Gullichsen • Robert Anton Wilson • Dr. Israel Regardie
Jeff Mandon • Osho • James Wasserman • Dr. Jack S. Willis
Dr. William S. Hyatt, Ph.D. • Lon Milo DuQuette • Chic & Tabatha Cicero
Richard Kaczynski, Ph.D. • David Cherubim • Steven Heller, Ph.D.
Daniel Pineda • Robert Brazil • Wayne Saalman • Peter Conte

NEW FALCON PUBLICATIONS
LOS ANGELES, CALIFORNIA, U.S.A.

Dedicated to
ALAN R. MILLER
A.K.A. CHRISTOPHER S. HYATT, PH.D.

Painting by Delfina Marquez-Noe

Obituary of
ALAN R. MILLER
A.K.A. CHRISTOPHER S. HYATT, PH.D.

From the *Los Angeles Times*, February 10, 2008

Alan Miller, Ph.D. passed into eternity on February 9, 2008 after his battle with cancer. Alan was born July 12, 1943, in Chicago, IL to Leonard Miller and Bertha Friedman. At seventeen-year-old he left high school and joined the U.S. Navy. Later he obtained his GED during his military service, and upon separation from the Navy, embarked upon his long and impressive academic journey.

His academic career began at Los Angeles City College. He then obtained a BA degree from Cal State Los Angeles, an MA in Psychology from Cal State Los Angeles, and Advanced M.Ed. from the University of Southern California, a Ph.D. in Psychology at Western University as well as other doctorate in human behavior from USIU. His specialty was in experimental and clinical psychology. He practiced as a psychotherapist for many years and operated his own clinic in Southern California.

Alan was an accomplished, and seaworthy sailor, who once embarked upon a journey to sail around the world. He founded and let the first AIDS Sailathon, which raised money for AIDS research by sailing from Long Beach, CA to Honolulu, HI in 1993. He was best known as an accomplished writer; writing under the pen name Christopher S. Hyatt, Ph.D. He authored more than 70 books, many of which pertained to the "Occult" and "Magick." His interest in the occult began in his early twenties. His desire to further pursue his studies in magick resulted in meeting Israel Regardie in the 1970s. Regardie introduced him to Reichian therapy and further instructed Alan in the magical system of the Hermetic System of the Golden Dawn.

Alan established the United States Ecclesiastical Society and Seminary to build a memorial library and spiritual center to preserve his work and honor that of Israel Regardie.

With Contributions from

Shelley Marmor

Lon Milo DuQuette

Jeff Mandon

Richard Kaczynski, Ph.D.

David Cherubim

James Wasserman

Osho (Bhagwan Shree Rejneesh)

Timothy Leary Ph.D.

Eric Gullichsen

Chic and S. Tabatha Cicero

Peter Conte

Christopher S. Hyatt, Ph.D.

Steven Heller, Ph.D.

Dr. Jack S. Willis

Dr. William S. Hyatt, Ph.D.

Dr. Israel Regardie

Robert Anton Wilson

Daniel Pineda

Robert Brazil

Wayne Saalman

Table of Contents

Foreword — xiii
Shelley Marmor

Preface — xvii
Lon Milo DuQuette

Introduction — xxvii
Jeff Mandon

Taboo and Transformation in the Words of Aleister Crowley — 1
Richard Kaczynski, Ph.D.

Foreword to The Eye in the Triangle — 15
David Cherubim

Pulling Liberty's Teeth — 27
James Wasserman

Rebellion Is The Biggest "YES" Yet — 51
Osho (Bhagwan Shree Rejneesh)

Twenty-Two Alternatives to Involuntary Death — 69
Timothy Leary Ph.D. and Eric Gullichsen

Theurgia Liberatio: Magic As Divine Liberation — 93
Chic and S. Tabatha Cicero

Team Psychopath — 115
Peter Conte

The Nature of Evil	125
from Aleister Crowley's Illustrated Goetia: Sexual Evocation *Lon Milo DuQuette and Christopher S. Hyatt, Ph.D.*	
Devil Be My God *Lon Milo DuQuette*	135
Breaking Trance *Steven Heller, Ph.D.*	139
The Black Art of Psychotherapy *Dr. Jack S. Willis*	141
Another Bedtime Story *Dr. William S. Hyatt, Ph.D.*	151
Ecstasy *Dr. Israel Regardie*	159
How Brain Software Programs Brain Hardware *Robert Anton Wilson*	171
The Rebel In Us All *Jeff Mandon*	187
Martial Arts: Path of Unification *Daniel Pineda*	201
Apocalypse Never? A Refutation of the Eschaton *Robert Brazil*	213
Angels, Devils, Spiritual Rebels *Wayne Saalman*	225
Authors	239

Foreword

Shelley Marmor

"Success is your proof; courage is your armour..."
–LiberAL vel Legis III:46

To say Dr. Christopher S. Hyatt, Ph.D. will not ever have mass appeal is an understatement. If anything, the masses detest him en masse. And rightfully so. His radical approach to self-transformation doesn't come sugarcoated or gift wrapped. Rather, Dr. Hyatt exposes every hypocrisy and forces his readers to face "yourselves as you are–not as you wish to be."[1] Because of this the Doctor is not for the truth-fearing majority, which worked out because he had no real interest in that demographic anyway.

In the Introduction to *The Psychopath's Bible: For the Extreme Individual* Dr. Hyatt writes about how many editors (which he calls "pencils for hire") refused to work on the book. Obviously the title is not a misnomer; the ideas contained in his book(s) are so extreme editors who earn a living editing books refused money to edit that one. And rightfully so! His work paints what for many is an all-too-real outlook of the human race, both in the microcosm of the individual and in the macrocosm of society. But what if Dr. Hyatt is right? What if the society we live in really is that Hobbesian after all? Either way, probably best to arm ourselves.

---

[1] Hyatt, Christopher S. *Undoing Yourself With Energized Meditation and Other Devices*. New Falcon Publications, 2010, pp.43.

In the world of Dr. Hyatt we formulate our ideas of ourselves and the world around us based on accumulated lies (aka "traditions") taught to us since childhood. As a result each person comes to believe in a fictitious "I" based solely on the liars in our lives regurgitating their lies onto us. "We are all handicapped by our traditions and conclusions,"[2] according to Dr. Hyatt. Heroically, and luckily for many of us, he does offer a way out.

Through his method of Undoing Yourself, and then formulating your new self, Dr. Hyatt teach how each of us can reclaim our thoughts, live on our own terms, and exceed what we thought our potential to be. Best of all he explains how you can turn tension back into energy–energy YOU direct as YOU see fit according to YOUR will. That's what the wicked Doctor, a clinical and experimental psychologist, offers his patient. Now why is that so wicked? Because as Dr. Hyatt said, "The 'you' which you are familiar with has been created through years of random, blind and unconscious programming. It is the result of happenstance, genetics and history. It has as much a relationship to your Real Self, as freedom to fascism."[3] In other words, at the end of the day we all have to transcend our-current-selves in order to become ourselves. No one is special and there are no exceptions; we have all been (forcibly) shaped by others and we all have to unlearn everything before we can become ourselves.

Make no mistake: dealing with yourself, changing everything you know, relearning how to be yourself, etc., *ad nauseam*, is a road paved with spikes, daggers, swords,

---

[2] Hyatt, Christopher S. *To Lie is Human: Not Getting Caught is Divine*. New Falcon Publications, 2006, p. 72.
[3] Hyatt, Christopher S. *Undoing Yourself With Energized Meditation and Other Devices*. New Falcon Publications, 2010, pp. 52-53.

and worst of all, mirrors. However, as Dr. Jack S. Willis aptly puts it, "If your objective is long term personal growth, then choose the teacher whose statements to you make you anxious, unsettled, nervous, unsure. Therein lies an answer."[4]

To put it another way Dr. Hyatt's books have the power to help make you become who you want to be or break you down even further. For those not broken, your personal Valhalla awaiting at the end of the rainbow, your YOU, is an unimaginable and unquantifiable reward.

At this point I feel I should say this is not my book report about Dr. Hyatt. This is what I learned from him and applied to my life to achieve personal change. It is a testimony that those who want to do the same can. More accurately, it is a declaration that those who want to do the same Will.

For those satiated enough in simply talking about personal transformation, Dr. Hyatt's work has little to offer aside from ingenious wit. His work is about action: doing something, doing anything, making progress, and forsaking the stagnation that led you to become the person you want to change.

His books and methodologies speak to the few and far between of existence–those who not only say they want to achieve self-actualization but who are willing to do *everything* it takes to achieve that end. Throughout Dr. Hyatt's work he repeatedly drills into the reader's head that this is not going to be easy. On the contrary, this process is going to hurt and it's going to leave a scar. He does, however, offer the probability that he "scar" will be the truest version of yourself to ever exist.

---

[4] Dr. Willis, Jack S. "The Black Art of Psychotherapy." See page 143.

Though he passed away in 2008, his take-no-prisoners approach to self-actualization lives on. The articles and essays contained in this book, many selected by Dr. Hyatt himself, were written by authors who carry the torch of the Doctor's great work including Peter Conte, Dr. Jack S. Willis, Steven Heller, Ph.D., and Dr. Hyatt's own son, William S. Hyatt. His personal friends and professional colleagues, Dr. Israel Regardie, Robert Anton Wilson, Timothy Leary, James Wasserman, Lon Milo Duquette and S. Jason Black, also contribute articles to this book. Many of these writers were considered "dangerous" (i.e. brutally honest). They are dangerous because they strip modern life and the human condition to their core, and they do it without fear or apology.

They take their place with the Lord of the Morning himself, Lucifer, as they traverse the terrain many dare not even think about. Lucifer, the Shining One, bravely reject imposed norms of acceptability to express their personal truth. We can only hope others will take our torch and carry it as they carve their own way through the jungle.

"Become who you are. There are no guarantees."
–Dr. Christopher S. Hyatt, Ph.D.

Preface

Lon Milo DuQuette

*Unthinking respect for authority
is the greatest enemy of truth.*
–Albert Einstein

Do what thou wilt shall be the whole of the Law.

My involvement in this unique and historic publication project began in late 1995 when my friend (and co-author on four book projects[1]), Alan R. Miller (aka Christopher S. Hyatt), called to say he wanted to take me out to dinner. I was a little hesitant to accept because we had a bit of a falling out a couple of years earlier and were speaking to each other as infrequently as possible. He invited me to choose the time and place so I picked a time and suggested The Arches in Newport Beach, one of the oldest (and most expensive) restaurants in the area. He said, "Done."

While drinking the best martinis in southern California we tried to recall exactly what had happened to sour our relationship. It didn't take long for us to remember that it was a boisterous night of being ruthlessly frank with each other–a slurred debate full of mutual observations of personal shortcomings spawned by too many of these damned martinis. After a silent moment or two of embarrassed reflection, we chose to sip white wine through the rest of the dinner.

---

[1] *Enochian World of Aleister Crowley, The Way of the Secret Lover, Aleister Crowley's Illustrated Goetia*, and *Taboo: Sex Religion and Magick*. All from New Falcon Publications.

We weren't meeting, however, to reminisce or patch up our friendship. He wanted to talk to me about a new project–an anthology of short works by some of the most controversial writers of the twentieth century including Dr. Timothy Leary, Robert Anton Wilson, Osho (Bhagwan Shree Rajneesh), and a host of other radical minds of the day.

It was a wonderful idea, and I told him so. After all, how many publishers go out of the way to present ideas that are viewed by the majority of our neighbors as being obscene, subversive, blasphemous, insane, and dangerous? The market for such a work is very small. I was flattered and a bit surprised when I was asked to contribute an article. I enthusiastically agreed. I had just the thing for the book.[2]

Compared with most of the other writers in this unique work my credentials might seem rather anemic. I was born in a pleasant suburb of Los Angeles in the late 1940s, raised in a pleasant (but woefully unconscious) small town in Nebraska, and, until my sophomore year in high school, never seriously labored in my mind about politics, religion, the nature of consciousness or the meaning (or the meaningless) of life.

The war in Vietnam (and the very real possibility that I would be drafted to fight and perhaps die for something I really didn't understand) served to underscore the importance of being awake while my classmates quietly sleep-marched into body bags. I had no idea where to begin this waking up process, but I knew I would have to do something, and fast. As it turned out, it would be something I decided *not* to do that put me on the fateful road to rebellion.

I was pondering my predicament as I took my seat in the high school auditorium and prepared to endure a patriotic

---

[2] *See* Devil Be My God.

convocation sponsored by the American Legion, and featuring greedy recruiters from the various branches of the Armed Services there to hungrily harvest a fresh crop of cannon fodder. Naturally, the convocation began with a color guard of Boy Scouts trooping the American flag to center stage. As if we were now in the presence of the Holy Grail, the unseen voice of Principal Boyd serenely ordered the assembly to stand up and recite the "Pledge of Allegiance to the Flag of the United States of America."

Now, please understand that I had always been proud to be an American and loved the principles (as much as a high school sophomore understood them) of our republic, and all those "freedoms" that I knew were not enjoyed by citizens of many other countries around the world. But the Pledge of Allegiance to the *Flag* had disturbed me from the moment I was bullied into taking part in the exercise in elementary school. Today something snapped. Today I said to myself 'fuck no!' I remained seated and silent during the pledge. No one seemed to notice...but I was wrong.

Later in the day I was stopped in the hall by Mr. Brown, a new social studies teacher from Colorado who had just been hired to replace his recently deceased predecessor. He said he noticed that I had not stood for the Pledge of Allegiance and asked me why. I told him I thought the whole things was stupid and that I resented the whole assembly's attempt to suck my naive classmates into a stupid-sounding war. I fully expected to get a lecture on what a nasty, unpatriotic little bastard I was. Instead, I got a warm smile and an invitation to visit him at his apartment after school.

Over cigarettes and coffee I learned a history of Vietnam conflict that I'd never heard before–a history that the rest of the world seemed to already know. I learned that there was a bigger world out there. I learned that there were many Americans, including Senators and Congressmen, who felt that our involvement in the war was a very un-American thing to do.

In the months that followed I received a world-class education in radical politics. I gathered a small cadre of my misfit friends to join me in these afternoon sessions with Comrade Brown. I started to collect anti-war buttons and bumper stickers, took a short correspondence course in draft counseling, and the dawn of my Junior year was putting it to use teaching lunch hour sessions in how to legally and illegally avoid the draft. This naturally brought down upon me the scorn of the school administration. I was expelled twice–once for refusing to cut my hair, the second time for the outrageously inappropriate charge of "sedition." "Sedition!" For high school draft counseling! Only in Nebraska. A couple of letters from the local Episcopal minister friend in the ACLU got me back in class in short order, but I was branded a cowardly and unpatriotic communist traitor.

By my senior year I was a card carrying rebel. I joined the *Student Peace Union*, the *Young People's Socialist League*, and the *Students for a Democratic Society*. To all but a couple of girlfriends and a close circle of fellow travelers, Lon the rebel had now become Lon the devil and the most despised student in Columbus High School. I loved it.

When it came time for me to register myself for the draft, I appeared at the Selective Service office sporting a green beret with a large "Fuck the Draft" button pinned front and center. I also carried with me a letter dated 1950 from the California doctor who originally diagnosed my Perthes hip disease. It read, "Lonnie cannot exercise below the waist." I brutally intimidated the sweet little wheelchair-bound lady at the SS office threatening that if I weren't classified 4-F or I-Y, I would claim Conscientious Objector status and cause so much trouble there would be hundreds of boys in town who would want to do the same thing. It was a ridiculous threat, but since World War I no one in Columbus, Nebraska ever talked to the Draft Board like that.[3]

Then one afternoon in the spring of 1966 I was searching for cigarettes in the drawer of our living room hutch when I discovered a letter from the U.S. Department of Justice in Washington D.C. It was addressed to my mother and included the address and telephone number of the FBI field office in Omaha and the name of an agent for her to contact. Mom was at work so I confronted my father.

The poor man was already barrel-chested and weak from the emphysema. He moved to the couch and started to clean his pipe and nervously tried to talk with me between carefully planned breaths.

"Your mother's worried about you. She thinks you're getting in with some pretty dangerous people. Her cronies at work told her she was being silly but she went ahead and wrote to the FBI. That's the letter she got back. She's already called the Omaha office and told them everything she thinks she knows."

I asked if he had heard her conversation, and he said, "Only the part where she told them that you've fallen in with Communists and that they were teaching you to hate your mother."

We both laughed.

---

[3] I don't know if the threat worked because immediately upon graduation I moved to California. Mail from Selective Service followed me for a while, but I just ignored them and threw them all away unopened. Finally the letters stopped coming. Could it have been that easy for everyone?

I still couldn't fathom what possessed her to do such a thing. I recalled only one occasion when my mother and I ever discussed politics. I drew her a picture of a bird with its wings spread to illustrate the various degrees of philosophies between the extreme left and the extreme right wings of American politics. It was a pleasant conversation (I thought) and pinpointed where FDR located on the wings and where Barry Goldwater and Lyndon Johnson were located on the big bird. I certainly didn't espouse any subversive or un-American sentiments. I guess the big bird just freaked her out.

Now she was freaking me out, because as innocent as my activities were, from the point of view of a wartime FBI investigation my activities might make me at least *appear* to be a person of interest.

I had taken a summer job delivering broken television sets to an Omaha electronics shop for repair. Each trip I had to wait there, sometimes up to five hours, before returning the 90 miles home with the repaired units. All that time in the big city enabled me to make contact with my urbane comrades in the peace movement, including several Episcopal priests and a Unitarian minister who introduced me to the aging former president of a large international labor union. This man, who had a son my age, was the most interesting character I had ever met. He was at the time an active member of the Progressive Labor Party, but for years was an organizer for the Communist Party U.S.A. He had pictures of himself with Cisco Houston and Woody Guthrie and Pete Seeger and the Weavers; he knew Gus Hall; he'd been shot in the back by strikebreakers in Dearborn, bitten by dogs in Selma, and jailed in Mississippi with Martin Luther King. I couldn't wait for Saturdays so I could visit this delightful page of walking history. I am sure if anybody was a target for domestic surveillance in those dark years it was my colorful commie mentor. But I was harmless enough. Nothing ever came from my involvement with the movement except a Washington dossier marked *Kids-so-wild-their-mothers-turn-em-in* or one for Mom labeled *Mothers-so-crazy-they-turn-in-their-kids*.

In the spring of 1966 I graduated from high school and instantly packed up and drove my blue 1960 VW van back to my Southern California birthplace and pretended to go to college. I registered at Orange Coast College of Costa Mesa. Officially, my major was Drama, but my real major was 'the 60s.' I immediately linked up with the local SDS whose off campus headquarters was a large two story old house in Costa Mesa.

Expecting to find the same kind of somber-faced, but work-shirted denizens of the new Left that populated the University of Nebraska, I instead was greeted by a cadre of some of the most beautiful young people that I had ever seen–surfer boys with sandy blonde locks, and the bra-less hippie goddesses with long straight hair and voices like Joan Baez. I was in teenage rebel heaven. I presented them with a homemade Viet Cong flag. They presented me with a pipe-load of hashish and an invitation to a lecture by the greatest (then) living rebel and devil of them all, Dr. Timothy Leary. My rebel life was about to take a radical turn…inward. But this is another story for another time.[4] I believe that it is safe to say that Dr. Leary's influence played a significant roll in shaping the lives, characters, attitudes, and ideas of the majority of the individuals who have contributed to this unique and historic publication.

---

[4] DuQuette, Lon Milo. *My Life With The Spirits*. Weiser Books: Boston, 1999.

In 1980, I and members of the O.T.O.[5] lodge in Newport Beach decided it was time that Dr. Leary received some kind of award–a token of appreciation for his influence upon the evolving consciousness of humanity. We named our award after one of the most infamous rebels and devils of them all, Adam Weisphaupt, the notorious founder of the Bavarian Illuminati. The plaque was laser etched on brass and mounted on heavy walnut. It was framed by the classic image of the Egyptian Goddess Nuit.

The inscription read:

O.T.O.
PEACE TOLERANCE TRUTH
SALUTATION ON ALL POINT OF THE TRIANGLE
Do what thou wilt shall be the whole of the Law.
THE GUILD OF ADVANCED THOUGHT (G∴O∴A∴T∴)
of
HERU-RA-HA LODGE O.T.O.
is honored to present to
DR. TIMOTHY LEARY
THE FIRST ANNUAL
ADAM WEISHAUPT ILLUMINATI AWARD
In recognition of incalculable service to Humanity and others. Because of his inspired research and courageous example, Dr. Leary Is directly responsible for raising the consciousness of our planet.
"YOUR ONLY ALLEGIANCE IS TO LIFE"
Love is the law, love under will.
Given this 11th day of July 1980 E.V.

---

[5] Ordo Templi Orientis (Order of the Temple of the East, or the Order of Oriental Templars) is an international fraternal and religious organization founded at the beginning of the 20th century. Originally it was intended to be modeled after and associated with Freemasonry, but under the leadership of Aleister Crowley was reorganized as a non-Masonic organization based on the Law of Thelema as its central religious principle. This Law–expressed as "Do what thou wilt shall be the whole of the Law" and "Love is the law, love under will"–was established in 1904 with the dictation of *The Book of the Law*.

After his death, this award was listed among the items sold by the auction house, Christie's in New York. If you are interested, you can still see a picture of it on Christie's website, Lot 13/Sale 8113.

In the years following, our lodge also presented the 'Illuminati Award' to two more rebels and devils whose work grace the pages of this book, Dr. Israel Regardie and Robert Anton Wilson. It is with a great deal of ironic amazement that I find my words bound between the covers of this remarkable book along with this new and dangerous generation of rebels and their counterparts who helped pave the way.

Love is the law, love under will.

Lon Milo DuQuette
Costa Mesa, California, November 15, 2008

Introduction

Jeff Mandon

When I was asked to write this introduction, frankly, I was thrilled; because so many of the authors I had sought to inform my thinking in the midst of my prolonged adolescence (which reached far into my 20s) are included here. I sought them to broaden my mind; to give me another side of things. Some of the thoughts they shared were quite radical; and time has done little to dampen them from being any less radical, nor less relevant. I would read these authors' thoughts and opinions, and share them (ham-handedly) with friends and parents; passing them off as my own just to try them out; to varying degrees of welcome. In short, these authors taught me how to think outside the box; and in the end to think for myself. I gobbled down their thoughts and opinions hungrily, because the long and short of it was that I was in rebellion. I guess I still am to some degree. It wasn't necessarily that I was in rebellion against my parents, or against society. I was in rebellion against myself.

I didn't know it then; I just knew I felt like I was outgrowing my skin and needed to shed it in order to survive and thrive. I was struggling to become myself. Far too often, someone had said to me, "just be yourself and everything will be fine." And I would panic, thinking to myself, "I wouldn't know where to begin." And I honestly didn't.

I knew enough to know that it wasn't my personality self that I wanted to be anymore. In fact, that was exactly what I was trying to get away from, because it was basically formed so much by defense mechanisms I had adopted growing up; and growing up scared; which I believe is becoming more and more prevalent among our youth today. Our society is currently infused with so much fear that it's very difficult for a full-grown adult, no less an adolescent, to avoid taking it in, and taking it in deeply.

They say there are only two emotions: Love and fear. Things like hatred, anger, jealousy, etc. are all fear-based when you really dig down deeply enough. I don't think anybody plans to rebel growing up. I mean it's not like you sit up one day and say, "Oh gee, I think I'll push everyone and anything away from me today that I find irritating or errant." And yet I think everyone; or at least most anyone who is worth knowing in the end, has rebelled at some point in their development.

Rebellion comes from deep inside, and I believe it comes when one's heart wakes. For it is then that you notice that so much of what you have been swallowing up to this point, no longer sits well with you. Your desire for liberty, for freedom; comes from deep inside now; as if it were placed there by God himself. And perhaps it is. For those of us who've answered its call, we know there is a price to be paid for that freedom; for that liberty. The price is rebellion, with all its attendant fallout. There's just no way of avoiding it. It's as if you've been renting an apartment all those years and you suddenly turn the light on one day, realize you are a home owner in fact, and you better start to know a little bit about how the lighting works in your home. How it's wired. What those pipes under the sink are all about.

We begin to explore ourselves inside independently. And many authors contained in this book helped shake me loose. In some ways forced me to spit out the candy I was beginning to choke on, that had been placed in my mouth by others far too long as a way of placating me. Because when you're struggling inside, you need to struggle 'til it's over. The gift you are given for this journey is choice. The ability to respond instead of merely react. When you are cognizant of the fact that you are always in choice, you will realize you are free.

Medicating it away doesn't work. Lord knows, I tried that for years; and by medicating I don't just mean medicine, or even drugs; but drinking, and shopping; gambling, watching mindless TV, reading insipid books; basically doing whatever you can to deny your own depths which can no longer pacify you when the heart is awakened. You certainly can't be happy; and on some level, you know it, if you're running that game. But you're willing to settle for a momentary distraction from your pain. A momentary distraction that you milk and moderate with your given magic substance, hoping you can make it last for years; which you can't.

Once you gain your freedom from your own inner fears, from your own blind spots; once you know, and I mean really know yourself enough that you can work on your defects of character as they arise, honestly and scrupulously; navigate your own way, with the sureness that comes from a deep dinner connection. That's freedom in this world. Because in your search within you, you find that it's not all bad news; and after all, isn't it that very fear, that kept you from exploring your inner depths for years?

There is a core of God within each and every one of us. And that spirit is of the light. As God is unalterable, so this part of him inside us follows suit; for it's no meager speck. God is indivisible for he is All, so this part of him inside you is full strength maximum-power God. And that Self is not a stranger to you; and yes, surrounding it there are rings of fear that growing up, met with trauma after trauma that you pushed aside, or buried, or failed to notice altogether managed to be the very source that placed them there. And that's your price of admission in reaching your core Self; your soul. But more often than not, as you explore the scary monsters that those rings of fear represent; you find those horrible faces that have so long frightened you, are just masks. And those rings of fear that kept you at bay for far too long, are just wounded children, scared themselves, who are looking for a way to defend against that mini-crucifixion they experienced.

I honestly think it's healthy to rebel at some point in your life. Rebellion is a journey home. It is the hero's journey. It's Dorothy in Oz. It's Luke Skywalker taking on Darth Vader. The hero journey is always worth exploring, because at any given time multitudes of people are experiencing it. The lucky ones overcome their demons and return heroes; but there are no guarantees. I grew up in the country; not every bird that is pushed out of the nest by its mother learns to fly before it hits the ground; but God bless the ones that do fly. They are role models for us all. The beautiful part is anyone and everyone can be a hero in their own life journey.

It doesn't matter the size of their life in terms of public exposure. You don't need to be on TV to be living at a ten. You can be home gardening and living at a ten. What matters is the striving. The earnest desire to be more and more your true Self.

That moment of crisis when you meet your demons is so vital; but let's face it, it's also very frightening. Something I finally learned, is that the difference between a breakdown and a breakthrough is whether you are spiritually alone or not. It's easy to isolate as you rebel in your youth or even in your adulthood; because it's never too late to become your true core Self, and after all, isn't that the point in the end? You can do it at any age, but if you're smart, young or old, you will not do it alone. A mentor is a beautiful thing; and anyone can be a role model for you; both positive and negative role models are all around us. And in any hero journey there are always friends to help keep you on the path and contribute to the final goal of coming home to yourself. And I do mean the Self that God created; not the one we made up to cover the vulnerability, the desire to love and be loved, honestly and deeply. The very one that seemed to have all those flaws when you're growing up, that in the end, turn out to be all the very qualities that you need to succeed in life; that is if you are going to live a life that recognizes the spiritual self that is you with equal shrift as that body and mind that is also you. That's the extraordinary thing about becoming your core self. Everyone around you will tell you how much you're changing, and that will be true; but for you, it will feel as if you are simply becoming your real true self, more and more. The self you always were deep inside, but were just too frightened or distracted or faithless to be.

It's all about the voice you listen to inside. Listen to the one that tells you to take heart; that tells you to be honest, especially with yourself. The one that knows there really is such a thing as magic and the truth, because you've heard it and felt it and know it; because your metaphysical and physical self, have told you so. Continue to discipline your mind, so that you release the thoughts of ego, which become more and more identifiable as you grow; and return to the thoughts of God which are your true thoughts. And remember we're not responsible for every ugly, vicious thought that flits through our mind. Don't let that distract you. We are responsible for those thoughts we detain; for those we nurture and cultivate.

Again, it simply about allowing yourself to be your best Self. Because there is a place of God within you that gives rise to your true Self, your true will, will come to match that of God. For they are literally coming from the same place. Your Sacred Heart. It starts when you ask, "What do I want?" And not satisfied with the answer, you ask instead, "No, what do I *really* want?" And you'll be surprised to find the answer is not shallow or greedy; but one of depth, for its coming from your heart. So, it's more than a shopping list; it's a longing; it's a dream you know you can make come true.

It is our nature to lean on something; and if we do not lean on God in this process, we are very likely to lean on something it would be best we not lean on. Oddly enough, when you lean on God, you actually gain a sense of independence in the world that is grounded and palpable; and people will see it and respond to it.

Whether you agree with them or not, this book is full of individualists; true mavericks. Men and women who went out on a limb, not as a goal, but just to live a life true to themselves; and living in truth is a way of life. Here they share their ideas; their wisdom; their truths. I hope you will find here a little inspiration and clarity. And the great thing is when you come back later to re-read this book you will be struck by wisdom you didn't catch the first time because you weren't at a place yet to utilize it. So, as you change, so does the book. May it help you grow. May it offer something you can take in right now that might change things for the better with you. And if you are stuck, may it inspire a rebellion in you; a Rebellion that will leave you better than you are; better than you thought you could be. Enough said. Go love.

Aleister Crowley (in 1906)
The Father of Modern Western Magick
Born 1875, Died 1947

TABOO AND TRANSFORMATION IN THE WORK OF ALEISTER CROWLEY
Richard Kacynski, Ph.D.

Spiritual polymorph, sexual omnivore, psychedelic pioneer, and unapologetic social misfit, Aleister Crowely cut a scandalous figure in his Edwardian heyday. He was rediscovered during the counter-cultural revolution of the 1960s and beatified as a pop culture icon, with the groundswell of interest resulting from his renaissance yet to crest. While his detractors are as numerous as his admirers, to dismiss him as a mere hedonist is to ignore the ghost in the machine: As Gerald Yorke, Crowely's friend and *advocatus diabolus*, explained: "Crowley didn't *enjoy* his perversion! He performed them to overcome his horror of them."[1] Yorke's is no disingenuous revisionist memoir. Throughout Crowley's corpus runs of the idea of spiritual transformation by plunging into one's phobias and philias.

The ceremonial magick championed by Crowley and his forebears in the Golden Dawn is, in a nutshell, alchemy: The transformation of one's base character into spiritual gold. Crowley sought to improve upon this High Art by channeling human nature's most powerful drives into a form of sexual alchemy. His rationale, while not using this language, boils down to a simple thesis: If psychological triggers can precipitate spiritual change, then the taboos socially programmed

---

[1] Fuller, Jeanne Overton. *The Magical Dilemma of Victor Neuburg*. London: W.H. Allen, 1965, p. 244.

into us can act as triggers for major spiritual transformation. Thus, Crowley spent his life probing the impulses against which guilt, sin or plain common sense dissuaded most. This behavior found its earliest expression in what Crowley admits is a defining moment of his childhood:

> I must have been about 6 years old. I was capering around my father during a walk through the meadows. He pointed out a branch of nettles in the corner of the field, close to the gate (I can see it quite clearly today!) and told me that if I touched them they would sting. Some word, gesture, or expression of mine caused him to add: Would you rather be told, or learn by experience? I replied, instantly, I would rather learn by experience. Suiting the action to the word, I dashed forward, plunged in the clump, and learnt.
>
> This incident is the key to the puzzle of my character.[1]

From there, the exploration of ill-advised impulses became a constant quest. Thanks to his fundamentalist upbringing in the Plymouth Brethren faith, an abundance of taboos presented themselves. Simply reading the wrong book was a potential misstep for the young Crowley. By his teenage years, he had discovered the "Three Evil Kings," i.e., Drin-King, Smo-King and Wan-King.

By the time Crowley entered Trinity College, he understood the hazards of gratuitous sensuality. His second book, the notorious *White Stains* (1898), emulated the Decadent art and literature of his social circle. Critics, then as well as today, twittered at such suggestive titles as "A Ballad of Passive

---

[1] Crowley, Aleister. Chapter LVII. Beings I Have Seen with My Physical Eye. *Magick Without Tears*. New Jersey: Thelema Publishing Co., 1954; rpt. Tempe, AZ: New Falcon Publications.

Aleister Crowley

Paederasty" and "With Dog and Dame," oblivious to the cautionary tale underlying the risqué subject matter: The book's protagonist finds the thrill of his mild erotic quirks waning over time, driving him to more extreme vices which ultimately culminates in madness and murder. At its core, the book is a critique of hedonism.

Despite the moral of *White Stains*, Crowley wrestled with his own young adult drives. Long periods of abstinence–

proscribed for magicians by medieval grimoires–proved counter-productive. While abstaining, sexual urges didn't dissipate, they consumed him. Rather than slowly starve the impulse to death, Crowley concluded a better strategy was simply to appease it and get on with the Great Work. He considered sex an impulse like thirst or hunger, best divorced from the emotional baggage which society attached to it. Later he would remark, "The stupidity of having had to waste uncounted priceless hours in chasing what ought to have been brought to the back door every evening with the milk!"[1] Alas, these countless priceless hours gained him a reputation whose repercussions he would suffer repeatedly throughout his lifetime: In 1900, on the basis of his character, he was barred from further advancement in the Hermetic Order of the Golden Dawn. Thus purposive indulgence collided with prudishness, and its eidolon was Queen Victoria.

Despite a childhood aversion to England's monarch, he admitted that "I was brought up in the faith that Queen Victoria would never die."[2] She symbolized the spirit of the age, where respectability and propriety was imposed on all expressions, both public and private. Social stagnation, Crowely believed, was rooted in this hypocritical and risible hyper-morality. It was in this context that Crowley and his climbing colleague, Oscar Eckenstien, "broke into shouts of joy and an impromptu war dance"[3] upon learning of Queen Victoria's death in 1901. By the time he wrote *The World's Tragedy* in February of 1909, his disdain had crystallized:

---

[1] Crowley, Aleister. *Confessions of Aleister Crowley*. London: Hill & Wang, 1969, p. 113.
[2] Chapter LXXVII. Work Worth While: Why? *Magick Without Tears*, See also an identical remark in *Confessions*, p. 41.
[3] *Confessions*, p. 216.

Priests who are celibates–outside of choir!
Maidens who rave in Lesbian desire:
The buck of sixty, cunning as a trapper,
Stalking the pig-tailed, masturbating flapper;
The creeping Jesus–Caution! we must shock it!_
With one hand through his turn-out breeches pocket;
Flagellants shrieking in our streets and schools,
Our men all hogs, and all our women ghouls:–
This is our England, pious dame and prude,
Who calls me blasphemous, unchaste, and rude![1]

By the end of 1909, Crowley began to realize the magical potential of sex. He was in Africa with his student Victor Neuburg, conducting a series of visionary experiments which would become *The Vision and the Voice*. While attempting to skry into the 14th of the 30 Enochian Aethyrs, Crowley found his progress blocked. Seized with inspiration, the magicians built a makeshift altar to the Greek god Pan and consecrated it with a sex act. Although Crowley was promiscuous, Neuburg was only his second male lover. The first, from his college days, left him with feelings of sin and guilt. This time, the homosexual encounter–in the open air under the desert sun, to the service of the Great Work– profoundly impacted him. He felt his ego–the Aleister Crowley raised in Victorian England by Plymouth Brethren parents–dissolve. In the language of initiation, he had crossed the Abyss.

Thus his attitude toward sex progressed significantly in the decade between entering college and writing *The Vision and the Voice*.[2] In his original view, the reproductive impulse was a distraction from spiritual work, and was best

---

[1] Crowley, Aleister. *The World's Tragedy*. Paris: privately printed, 1910, p. XXXVII; 2nd ed. Phoenix: New Falcon Publications, 1992.

[2] Crowley, Aleister. Liber LX: The Ab-ul-Diz Working. *The Vision and the Voice with Commentary and Other Papers*. York Beach: Weiser, 1998, p. 287-337.

sated to maximize the amount of time the mind could devote to higher goals. By 1909, he realized that the socially constructed boundaries called morality could literally block spiritual growth. By breaching taboos, Crowley realized he could break down these barriers, countermanding his social programming. This is what a later generation of rebels and devils would call "undoing yourself."[1]

Crowley's 1912 meeting with Theodor Reuss, head of the Ordo Templi Orientis, forged the last link in this chain of thought. In this legendary encounter, Reuss accused Crowley of revealing the O.T.O's central secret in *The Book of Lies*. When Crowley claimed innocence, Reuss directed him to Chapter 36, *"The Star Sapphire."* Reading the words, "Let the Adept be armed with his Magick Rood [and provided with his Mystic Rose]" with the understanding that Reuss interpreted these words as sexual symbols, the light bulb lit. The chain was completed. Sex was not merely a distraction from the Great Work, nor merely a barrier to advancement. It was the very vehicle of a potent form of magick which replaced the traditional claptrap with our own bodies.

To be fair, Crowley was already heading in this direction, as documented in the Abuldiz working, The *Scented Garden*, and *Liber Stellae Rubeae*.[2] But the Reuss encounter gathered those thoughts into coherent form. From this point, Crowley vigorously engaged not only in ritual sex[3] but other taboo experiences, all in the pursuit of spiritual insight.

---

[1] Hyatt, Christopher S. *Undoing Yourself with Energized Meditation and Other Devices*. 6th printing. Tempe, AZ; New Falcon Publications, 1993.
—— *Undoing Yourself Too*. Tempe, AZ; New Falcon Publications, 1998.
[2] *The Scented Garden of Abdullah the Satirist of Shiraz*, (Bagh-i-muattar). London, 1910:rpt Chicago: Teitan Press, 1991.
—— Liber Stellae Rubeae sub figura LXVI. *The Equinox I*, (7). 1912, p. 29-36.
[3] Symonds, John, and Grant, Kenneth. (eds). *The Magical Record of the Beast 666*. Quebec: Next Step, 1972; rpt. London: Duckworth, 1983.

Thus, when he took up painting around 1917, he advertised for "Dwarfs, Hunchbacks, Tattooed Women, Harrison Fisher Girls, Freaks of All Sorts, Coloured Women only if exceptionally ugly or deformed, to pose for artist." When he founded his Abbey of Thelema in Cefalù, Italy, in 1920, he took a page from Paul Gaugin and made the walls his canvas. The result was *La Chambre des Cauchemas* (Chamber of Nightmares), whose murals bombarded viewers with an array of frightful, disturbing and sexually explicit images. Crowley told visitors:

> There, in the corner, are Lesbians as large as life. Why do you feel shocked and turn away: or perhaps overtly turn to look again? Because, though you may have thought of such things, you have been afraid to face them. Drag all such thoughts into the light... 'Tis only your mind that feels any wrong... Freud endeavors to break down such complexes in order to put the subconscious mind into a bourgeois respectability. That is wrong–the complexes should be broken down to give the sub-conscious will a chance to express itself freely..."[1]

Karl Germer, visiting the Abbey in 1926, confirmed the cathartic intent of these murals. "Beast evidently did all that as a medicine...against the English disease *par excellance*."[2]

Having fleshed out his psychological theory of magick, he began explaining it to his students. As Frank Bennett recounts his visit to Cefalù,

---

[1] Captain J.H.E. Townsend to J.F.C. Fuller, 19 April 1921, Harry Ransom Humanities Research Center, University of Texas at Austin.
[2] Karl Germer to Norman Mudd, 4 February 1926, Binder New 116, Yorke Collection, Warburg Institute, University of London.

> [H]e began to talk about initiation, and said it was a matter of getting the sub-conscious mind at work, that when this subconscious mind was allowed to have full sway, without interference with the physical mind, illumination began for he said this subconscious mind was our Holy Guardian. He illustrated this by saying that everything was felt in this mind, and it is constantly urging its will upon the physical mind, and when these impressions, or inner desires, are restricted or suppressed, evil and all kind of trouble are the result.[1]

While Crowley disagreed with psychoanalysis,[2] this etiological theory or "evil and all kind of trouble" paraphrases Freud's ideas regarding repression, sublimation and neurosis.

He also experimented with drugs at this time, making them accessible to the Abbey's visitors to rob them of their mystique and allure. His view on drug addiction paralleled *White Stains*' warning about sex, and, by extension, apply to all behaviors driven by the pleasure principle: Anything pursued hedonistically ultimately leads to moral collapse; but placing it in service to the Will protects the magician from addiction or other apostasies.[3] This calls to mind *The Book of*

---

[1] Frank Bennett. (1921). Magical Record of Frater Progradior in a Retirement at. Cefalu Sicily. Yorke Collection.

[2] Crowley, Aleister. An improvement upon psychoanalysis. *Vanity Fair*, December 1916, p. 60, 137; rpt. Hymenaeus Beta and Richard Kaczynski (eds.)., *The Revival of Magick and Other Essays*. Tempe, AZ: New Falcon, 1998.

[3] Crowley, Aleister. *The Diary of a Drug Fiend*. London: W. Collins & Co., 1922.

——. The great drug delusion. A New York Specialist (pseud.) *The English Review*, July 1922, p. 65-70.

——. The drug panic. A London Physician (pseud). *The English Review*, (7). 1912, p. 29-36.

——. Crowley found these principles harder than expected to put into practice in *Liber Tzaba vel Nike (The Fountain of Hyacinth)*, Binder A4-A5, Yorke Collection.

the Law's instruction, "To worship me take wine and strange drugs whereof I will tell my prophet, & he be drunk thereof! They shall not harm ye at all." (*AL* ii.22). On this passage, Crowley cautioned:

> Lest there be folly, let me say that this passage does not license reckless debauch. The use of drugs and drink is to be strictly and act of Magick. Compare what is said in the First Chapter with regard to the use of the functions of sex.[1]

Thus he reiterated that explorations of the human psyche's dark underbelly be intentional and purposive.

Other experiments at Cefalù involved gender bending, the *menage a trois*, sado-masochism and coprophagia. While Crowley considered this legitimate psychological research, he realized the controversial nature of his work. Between the publication of *The Diary of a Drug Fiend* and the unfortunate death from typhoid of an Abbey visitor, the tabloids of the time unleased an astonishing series of attacks. Crowley's reaction:

> I regard all these people, all England with rare individual exceptions, as moral cowards with all that that implies. Sir Richard Burton had an experience precisely similar to mine. So had Christopher Columbus. So had Darwin. Their instinctive dread of a man who dares the unknown. *Omne Ignotum pro terribili* and such a man may bring it to their door at any moment. The whole history of science illustrates this. Science is now tolerated because Science has been at pains to prove that (on the balance) it has benefited mankind. I, bringing as I do, new knowledge of the unknown, and obviously the mark of fear, horror and persecution.[2]

---

[1] Crowley, Aleister. Duplicate typescript with mss corrections of part of the unpublished commentary on the 'Book of the Law,' Oasis of Nefta, Al-Djerid, Tunisia, 1923. Rare Books Department, Z. Smith Reynolds Library, Wake Forest University, Winston-Salem, N.C.

[2] Aleister Crowley to Norman Mudd, 20 April 1924, Yorke Collection.

Small wonder that Crowley's records from Cefalù were seized and destroyed by H.M. Customs as pornographic when he tried returning them to England.

In the end, Crowley became the eidolon or reflection of those impulses denied by society which Queen Victoria symbolized. Confronting the Beast meant confronting those repressed impulses, with the resulting ordeal dubbed "The Vision of the Demon Crowley." Indeed, those who persevered and saw through the smoke screen became his staunchest advocates–Gerald Yorke, Louis Wilkinson, Karl Germer and Israel Regardie among them–while those who bolted off were convinced they had narrowly escaped the clutches of the devil. "The main danger seems to be getting caught on the reef of his own interpretation," Kenneth Grant commented. "But this, after all, is but the proper function of the 'Demon Crowley'!"[1] Likewise, when Crowley began a campaign to rehabilitate his reputation, Gerald Yorke neatly summarized the function of the Great Beast:

> To my mind, part of your 'mission,' if I may use a word I mistrust, is to show that the code of morals of what a Thelemite calls the Old Aeon has been superseded, and that now any act is right provided it is done in the right way, as in interpretation of True Will. It must have been your Will to be the Beast, and a whitewashed Beast is an useless commercial article.[2]

Crowley must have been convinced, for he continued living the rest of his life with no apologies.

---

[1] Kenneth Grant, private communication, 5 December 1989.
[2] Gerald Yorke to Aleister Crowley, 20 March 1928, Binder New 116, Yorke Collection.

Aleister Crowley
Also known as
*The Beast 666, The Wickedest Man Alive
and The Prophet of the New Aeon*

Analogues in Other Traditions

The notion of sacrifice–literally to make sacred, or to find the holy in the mundane–is not unique to Crowley.

Hasidic Jews find God through the "enjoyable and necessary acts of ordinary life."[1] Early forms of Hasidism's *Chabad* mysticism included practices like *Haalat ha-Nitzotzot* ("elevating the sparks," or recognizing everything as a manifestation of God), *'Avodah he-Hipukh* ("worship through inversion," where self-fulfillment comes from joining things–even God–with its opposite), and its extension *Yeridah Le-Tsorekh 'Aliyah* ("descent for the purpose of ascent"). When the *Tzaddikim* began discussing things like

---

[1] Cantor, Norman F. The Sacred Chain: The History of the Jews. New York: Schocken, 1988.

the sanctity of sin, exploring the *Sitra Ahra* (the "opposite tree" or *Qlippoth*), or discussing how one can find God by exploring the desire to kill one's neighbor, these practices were eliminated as dangerous.[1]

In Tantra, followers of the *Kaula* branch and *vama marg* or "left hand path" advocate the well-known *panchamakaras* or *panchatattva* ritual. Literally meaning "five elements," it involves partaking five substances which are usually religiously prohibited. The five items, in Sanskrit, all begin with the letter M; hence, this ritual is often referred to as "the five M's." The items are *madya* or *madir*–(wine or liquor), *matsya* (fish), *m–msa* (meat), *mudr*–(parched grain) and *maithun*–(sex, often out of caste). The concept behind this ritual is that which drove Crowley's explorations: Social taboos, broken in a religious context, can produce great spiritual advancement.[2]

Finally the masters known as the Aghori represent such an extreme manifestation of this formula that they are the object of fear and awe in India, believed to have transcended all boundaries of good and evil. Their best-known activities center around mankind's greatest taboo, death. *Aghori* will sleep in cemeteries, often sharing the same coffin with

---

[1] Ariel, David S. *The Mystic Quest: An Introduction to Jewish Mysticism*. New York: Schocken, 1988. Elior, Rachel. *The Paradoxical Ascent to God: The Kabbalistic Theosophy of Habad Hasidism*. New York: State University of New York Press, 1993.

[2] Garrison, Omar. Tantra: *The Yoga of Sex. New York*: Causeway, 1964. Geuerstwin, Georg. *Tantra: The Path of Ecstasy*. Boston: Shambhala, 1998. Douglas, Nik, and Slinger, Penny. *Sexual Secrets: The Alchemy of Ecstasy*. New York: Destiny, 1979; rpt. New York: Inner Traditions.

corpses. They observe and wait, ready to celebrate the popping of the body's skullcap, for to them that represents the final release of the soul. Once or twice in a lifetime, an *Aghori* will consume a piece of human brain, the first place to show the stirrings of the spirit and the last place from which it is vacated. Even necrophilia is not unknown.[1] By immersing themselves in the most dreaded of all things—human death and decay—the *Aghorii* seek not only to come to terms with death, but also—like Crowley, the *Chabad* mystics and the *Tantrikas*—to come a little closer to understanding God.

---

[1] Svoboda, Robert E. *Aghora: At the Left Hand of God*. Brotherhood of Life: Albuquerque, NM, 1986.

Aleister Crowley, circa 1906

"I also am a Star in Space, unique and self-existent, an individual essence incorruptible; I also am one Soul; I am identical with All and None. I am in All and All in Me; I am, apart from all and lord of all, and one with all"
—Aleister Crowley

Foreword to
THE EYE IN THE TRIANGLE
An Interpretation of Aleister Crowley
by Israel Regardie
New Falcon Publications, Eleventh Printing 2022

David Cherubim
Aleister Crowley Foundation
Los Angeles, California U.S.A. Aug. 31, 2001 e.v.

Do what thou wilt shall be the whole of the Law.

Aleister Crowley, the *Great Beast 666*, was a passionate poet, prolific writer, daring mountaineer, and master occultist. He was born on October 12th, 1875 in Leamington Spa, Warwickshire, England, and he passed away into the Infinite at the green old age of 72 on December 1st, 1947 at Netherwood in Hastings. Since his death, his influence on magicians and mystics, musicians, writers and artists of all sorts, has been very significant. The music scene, in particular, has been, and continues to be, the most fertile ground for Crowley's name and teachings, and it has gained the *Great Beast 666* more recognition than any other artistic field. Some of the most successful musicians we know have studied, practiced or praised the works of Aleister Crowley and his *Law of Thelema*.[1] It is rather remarkable that in such a short time after his death Crowley should have attained to

---

[1] The *Law of Thelema* is "Do what thou wilt shall be the whole of the Law. Love is the law, love under will."

[2] The Thelemic community is composed of Thelemites, that is, individuals who practice the *Law of Thelema*.

such a lofty level of influence. As one who has been involved with the Thelemic community[2] since the days when that only consisted of a handful of Thelemites here and abroad, to watching it expand into a virtual subculture, I am deeply moved by this needed growth of events, since it has also been so much a part of my True Will to help *Thelema* expand and to perpetuate the teachings of Aleister Crowley. To this end I started the *Aleister Crowley Foundation*.[3]

At the age of twenty, I obtained my first copy of *The Eye in the Triangle* at an Occult Bookstore in Los Angeles called *The Psychic Eye* and, naturally, I read it with the greatest enthusiasm and interest, and I excitedly extracted the essentials from its pages. It subsequently left a deep impression upon my mind, and it has continued to influence my life in ways invaluable to my growth as both a man and a magician. Since that first reading, I have read the book a few more times, including recently, and every time it has illumined my understanding of Crowley, his magick and his mysticism in some manner or another useful to my life and magical progress. I have read most published and unpublished works by Israel Regardie, but this

---

[3] The Aleister Crowley Foundation was started in 1998 e.v. and it is maintained by David Cherubim in association with the *Thelemic Order of the Golden Dawn* which was founded by David Cherubim *(Frater Aurora Aurea)* and Christopher S. Hyatt *(Frater Adonai Achad)* on the Vernal Equinox of 1990 e.v. in Los Angeles, CA, USA. Israel Regardie (November 17th, 1907 e.v. – March 10th, 1985 e.v.) initiated his close friend, student and publisher Christopher S. Hyatt, Ph.D. (July 12th, 1943 e.v. – February 9th, 2008 e.v.) in the Golden Dawn. Dr. Hyatt later initiated David Cherubim as an Adept in the Golden Dawn (or more accurately in the Second Order called the *Rosae Rubeae et Aureae Crucis*) on March 10th, 1990 e.v., five years after Regardie's death, to carry on Regardie's lineage of the Golden Dawn. David Cherubim also maintains the Israel Regardie Foundation which was originally established by the late Christopher S. Hyatt who, with Regardie's assistance, also founded Falcon Press (New Falcon Publications).

book is the one he wrote that moved me the most, finding the greatest meaning and place in the sanctuary of my soul. I feel that *The Eye in the Triangle* is essential reading material for anyone who is seriously interested in learning about the life, magick and mysticism of Aleister Crowley.

It is true that Regardie did not always have the most objective interpretations or ideas about Crowley and his character–even calling him once a contemptible bitch!–and that he projected unto Crowley some of his own weaknesses, but this is true of most effective relationships of this kind, that is, among gurus and their chelas, teachers and their students, psychotherapists and their clients, and so on, and Regardie later recognized the reality of this psychological process that took effect within him. The fact is, Crowley was his spiritual mentor. Regardie once stated during an interview, "Crowley somehow had an enormous maturing effect on me. I was a young boy when I met him, I had just turned 20. Somehow, in his own inimitable way, he helped me to grow up and become something of an adult. I owe him a very, very great deal, a very great deal. Later we fell out, which was due to my own stupidity. After I recovered my annoyance of a quarrel with him, I reestablished my admiration for him, and my love, if you like, and still hold him in the highest esteem, although I am a great deal more objective about him now than I ever was before."[4]

Israel Regardie (November 17th, 1907 – March 10th, 1985), referred to as "the Serpent" by Crowley, met with the *Great Beast 666* in Paris in October of 1928 to become his

---

[4] From *An Interview with Israel Regardie: His Final Thoughts and Views* (Falcon Press, 1985).

[5] At the back of this book is a copy of a letter from Aleister Crowley dated June 12th, 1930, introducing Israel Regardie as his Secretary and Confidential Agent, as well as a copy of a Postcard from Aleister Crowley (729) sent to Israel Regardie, addressing Regardie as a Ninth Degree member of the O.T.O. (Ordo Templi Orientis).

personal secretary and student (he also became Crowley's Confidential Agent and a IX° Member of Crowley's O.T.O.).[5] On October 28, 1930, Regardie took the Oath of the Probationer in Crowley's Order of the A∴A∴ (*Astron Argon*). The Order of the A∴A∴ was Crowley's reformulated and advanced version of the system of the Golden Dawn (Crowley even maintained the name of the Golden Dawn for the Outer Order, or the *Aurora Aurea*). Then in January of 1933, shortly after severing with Crowley, Regardie, like his magical mentor, joined the Golden Dawn (or, more appropriately, an offshoot of the Order called the *Stella Matutina*) at Hermes Temple in Bristol with the Neophyte motto Frater *Ad Majorem Adonai Gloriam.*[6] Regardie states in this book, *The Eye in the Triangle*, that he retained this same Neophyte Motto for his 5=6 Adept degree, the Adeptus Minor Grade. This book is the work of an Adept who was devoted to the Great Work of preserving and perpetuating the teachings of both Aleister Crowley and the Golden Dawn about which he once stated: "They have left indelible marks on my life, and my career if I want to use that term, but certainly on my personal life. On the other hand, I cannot separate Crowley from The Golden Dawn, because Crowley was *The Golden Dawn and The Golden Dawn was Crowley*."[7]

Aleister Crowley joined the *Hermetic Order of the Golden Dawn* on November 18th, 1898 as a Neophyte (0=0)

---

[6] A phrase meaning, "To the greater glory of my Lord."
[7] From *An Interview with Israel Regardie: His Final Thoughts and Views* (Falcon Press, 1985).
[8] Frater is a Latin word meaning "Brother," and Perdurabo is a Latin word meaning "I will endure." Taking this magical motto entailed that Crowley would endure unto the end of the initiatory system of the Golden Dawn. This, of course, he accomplished in his lifetime, taking the great oath of the final grade of Ipsissimus on May 23rd, 1921 e.v.

with the magical motto Frater *Perdurabo*.[8] Naturally, Crowley advanced quickly in the Order. As a Neophyte, he was initiated to the next grade of Zelator (1=10) in December of 1898, as a Theoricus (2=9) in January of 1899, as a Practicus (3=8) in February of 1899, and as a Philosophus (4=7) in May of 1899. He then took his Portal Initiation in December of 1899, and he was then initiated as an Adeptus Minor in Paris on January 16th, 1900 by S. L. MacGregor Mathers, who was the Chief of the Order at that time, and whom Crowley first met in May of 1899.

Now scandal and schism arose in the Order in 1900; the London Adepts were in revolt against Mathers, the Chief of the Order; and by the end of March, the London Temple declared independence from Mathers. Crowley originally sided with Mathers during the revolt, but he then went on his own merry way to Mexico and he became a Freemason. Crowley stated, "In 1900, the Order in its existing form was destroyed."[9]

Then on April 8th, 9th and 10th of 1904 e.v., between noon and 1 p.m., Crowley received *The Book of the Law* (Liber Legis). This book was dictated to Crowley in Cairo by a Praeter-human Intelligence named Aiwass whom Crowley later came to recognize as his own Holy Guardian Angel. The book proclaimed that Crowley was the Prophet of a New Æon (New Age). As such, he later became the founder of a New Order, which he called the Order of the A∴A∴, maintaining the name of the Golden Dawn (*Aurora Aurea*) as the title of the Outer Order. In this book, *The Eye in the*

---

[9] From The Book of Thoth (The Equinox Vol. III, No. V) by the Master Therion (Aleister Crowley). This book was originally published in 1944 as a limited edition (200 numbered and signed copies). It was first reprinted by Samuel Weiser in 1969.

Triangle, Israel Regardie states the following fact regarding Crowley, "All his work is a direct continuation of the Golden Dawn tradition." He also states the following, "Beyond all other mundane events it was the influence of the Hermetic Order of the Golden Dawn that shaped Aleister Crowley's life. Once exposed to its Qabalistic system of grades and philosophy, its magical practices and ceremonies, he was never the same."

Aleister Crowley's reception of *The Book of the Law* was a direct manifestation and result of his initiation in the Golden Dawn. The Golden Dawn was, in fact, the basis of the Proclamation of the *New Æon of Horus* and the *Law of Thelema*. After receiving The Book of the Law, Crowley wrote and sent a letter to his initiator, S. L. MacGregor Mathers, informing him that the Secret Chiefs had appointed him (Crowley) to be the visible Head of the Order of the Golden Dawn. Mathers, of course, did not respond, but nor did Crowley expect a response from him.

On July 27th, 1906 Crowley renewed his Adeptus Minor obligation during a visit with another Adept of the Golden Dawn, George Cecil Jones (1873-1953). It was Jones who proposed to Crowley that he join the Golden Dawn and he sponsored Crowley for his Neophyte initiation on November 18th, 1898. On July 29th, 1906 these two Adepts of the Golden Dawn discussed the idea of forming a New Order. Crowley recorded the following in his diary: "D.D.S. and P. discuss a new O." By December 10th, 1906 Jones recognized Crowley as a Magister Templi (Master of the Temple). Crowley, however, did not actually accept this exalted spiritual grade until December 3rd, 1909. But by their sincere efforts and spiritual preparation a New Order was made manifest in the year 1907, called the Order of the A∴A∴ (*Astron Argon*). Later Crowley rightfully violated his Oath of Secrecy to the *Hermetic Order of the Golden Dawn* and published its rituals and teachings in his prodigious periodical called *The Equinox*, which Crowley published to help preserve the Sacred Tradition, so that a new Renaissance might in due season rekindle the Hidden Light.

On April 21st, 1912, Crowley also became the National Grand Master General X° of the O.T.O.[10] for Great Britain and Ireland. His charter was issued by one of the co-founders of the O.T.O., Theodor Reuss,[11] who accused Crowley of publishing sexual secrets of the IX° of the O.T.O., though Crowley protested such an accusation, not even knowing to what he was referring. However, this peculiar event developed into a conversation between these two men, deeply arousing Crowley's interest in the O.T.O. which he had already joined in 1910, and Reuss gave Crowley an O.T.O. charter. Then in 1922, Crowley became the O.H.O. (Outer

---

[10] O.T.O. are the initials for *Ordo Templi Orientis* (Order of the Eastern Temple or Order of the Temple of the East). The official website for the O.T.O. is at http://www.oto-usa.org.

[11] Theodor Reuss (1855-1923) was associated with William Wynn Westcott (1848-1925), a London Coroner, Theosophist, Freemason and Rosicrucian, who was the primary founder of the *Hermetic Order of the Golden Dawn* and the Supreme Magus of the *Rosicrucian Society of England* (Societas Rosicruciana in Anglia, or Soc. Ros.). Theodor Reuss received a charter (dated July 26th, 1901) from William Wynn Westcott for the Swedenborgian Rite of Masonry, and he also received from Westcott a letter of authorization (dated February 24th, 1902) to found a High Council in Germania of the Societas Rosicruciana in Anglia.

Head of the Order). Under Crowley, the system of the O.T.O. was reconstructed to promulgate in the world the Law of Thelema and the principles of *The Book of the Law*.

After his death, Crowley's work influenced the creation of another prominent Occult Order, called the *Thelemic Order of the Golden Dawn*,[12] which was founded on the Vernal Equinox of 1990 by two members of the O.T.O. and Golden Dawn. The initiation ceremonies of this Order were constructed to accord with the principles of *The Book of the Law* and to instruct the Initiate in the *Magick of Thelema*, for the realization of his or her True Will, and for the attainment of the Knowledge and Conversation of his or her Holy Guardian Angel. The central teaching of Aleister Crowley derives from *The Book of the Law* (Liber Legis), which announces to mankind the *New Æon of Horus* that commenced on the Vernal Equinox of 1904 e.v., and which shall remain for a period of 2,000 years. After its dictation, Crowley dismissed *The Book of the Law* as being of no great value and in the course of time he simply lost the original manuscript. It was not until five years after its dictation that he inevitably came across it, and this without the conscious intent to do so. It was after this event that Crowley began to seriously study and comprehend *The Book of the Law*.

---

[12] The *Thelemic Order of the Golden Dawn*, also called the Order of the T∴G∴D∴ (Thelemic Golden Dawn), is the *Novus Ordo Aurora Aurea* (New Order of the Golden Dawn). The official website for the *Thelemic Order of the Golden Dawn* is at http://www.thelemicgoldendawn.net.

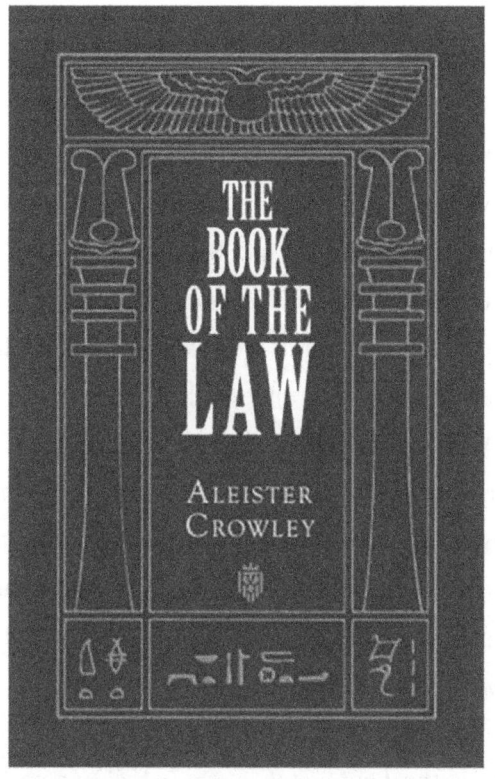

Aiwass, the Angel who dictated *The Book of the Law*, claimed to be "the minister of Hoor-Paar-Kraat." Hoor-Paar-Kraat (Harpocrates in Greek mythology) is the Egyptian God of Silence. Crowley came to identify *Aiwass* as one of the Secret Chiefs or Hidden Masters of the A∴A∴, a discarnate entity of superhuman intelligence and power. The A∴A∴ is the secret Invisible Order of the Universe, and *Aiwass* is the principal Messenger from that Interior Order at this aeonic stage in our spiritual evolution. The God symbolic of the Third Order is Hoor-Paar-Kraat, or

Harporcrates, the Lord of Silence. Hoor-Paar-Kraat is the Babe in the Egg of Blue, or the Crowned Child upon the Lotus, and He is a universal symbol of the Holy Guardian Angel. He represents the Secret Self of every man and every woman, that is, their Silent Self or Holy Guardian Angel. True understanding of this Silent Self is the Universal Key to every mystery of Magick and Mysticism.

The central message of *The Book of the Law* is the *Law of Thelema*: "Do what thou wilt shall be the whole of the Law. Love is the law, love under will." Thelema is the Greek word for Will. It–like Agape, the Greek word for Love–has the numerical value of 93. In the Qabalah there is a numerological system called Gematria, which informs us that words with the same numerical value are descriptions of each other or they are indications of a single phenomenon. The *Law of Thelema* is the Law of Will and Love. Every act of Love must be under Will, that is, in accordance with one's True Will. Such is the *Law of Liberty* by which we perfect ourselves in Nature to realize and accomplish our True Will.

The magical doctrine of *The Book of the Law* asserts that every man and every woman has a proper course in life–a True Will–just as every star has its own orbit, and that the duty of every individual is to pursue his or her own course, just as every star must move on its own orbit. *The Book of the Law* proclaims: "Every man and every woman is a star." We are all individual Centers of the Universe, each with our own unique Path to pursue in the Cosmic Order. As such, we are to be free of all standard ways and codes of conduct, and we are to exist by our own inward light and truth in this *Way of Liberty*. If we all did our True Will there would be no conflict and no interference with one another. The *Book of the Law* further states that we have no right but to do our Will, and that any deviation from this path is a direct violation of the *Law of Thelema*. We must know our True Will and do it with one-pointedness, and without lust of result. Also every act is to be a sacrament, a ritual of *Love under Will*. It may all be summed up in one simple injunction: There is no law beyond *Do what thou wilt*. Such was the message of Aleister Crowley, the *Great Beast 666*.

Love is the law, love under will.

David Cherubim
August 31st, 2011 e.v.

James Wasserman

Lord, I thank You for my creation
I acknowledge that I am a star
Whose orbit and purpose I am
pledged to follow and pursue
Free me from bondage of false selves
That I may know and do my True Will
To the glory of Thine Ineffable Name
AUMGN

PULLING LIBERTY'S TEETH

James Wasserman

"A well regulated Militia, being necessary to the security of a free State, the right of the people to keep and bear Arms, shall not be infringed."
-Second Amendment to the U.S. Constitution

"Those who beat their swords into plowshares will do the plowing for those who didn't."
-Self-Evident Fact of Life

A "MILLION" MISINFORMED MOMS

To paraphrase a famous gun-controller of old, May 14, 2000 is "a date which will live in infamy." A group consisting mostly of women and estimated at between 150,000 and 500,000, forewent the traditional family pleasures associated with the annual Mother's Day holiday to rally around TV personality and former Kmart spokeswoman Rosie O'Donnell. She was accompanied by such well-known gun confiscation luminaries as Diane Feinstein, Maxine Waters and Sarah Brady, all of whom spent the day expressing their contempt for the aspirations of America's founders, and their disdain for law-abiding Americans who believe in the Second Amendment. It was the first time in this writer's memory that a mass protest was aimed directly at the Bill of Rights.

Many of the "Moms" at the march were undoubtedly veterans of the Anti-War movement of the 1960s and 70s, when the youthful idealism of a generation was masterfully manipulated by the anti-American Left. Now in middle-age, those who never woke up to the assault on Liberty embodied by the Nanny State, bared their teeth for a direct attack against the hated "rich, white, slave-owning men" who built the greatest, most prosperous, and freest nation in the history of the world. Professor Camille Paglia describes the march as "... the gun control protest organized (as the major media is finally admitting) by the sister-in-law of Hillary Clinton's longtime lawyer pal and hatchet woman, surly Susan Thomases..."[1] Surprised?

THE SECOND AMENDMENT: AN INDIVIDUAL RIGHT?

The "shot heard round the world" was fired during the first battle of the American Revolution on April 19, 1775 at British soldiers seeking to enforce British gun control laws by confiscating weapons and gunpowder belonging to the citizens of Concord, Massachusetts. Both Dr. Joyce Lee Malcolm in *To Keep and Bear Arms* and Dr. Stephen P. Halbrook in *That Every Man Be Armed* have provided prodigious, compelling and common sense scholarship to prove that the Second Amendment is a right possessed by the people[2]. If the reader has any doubt of this, he or she is referred to these two scholars. On the other hand, the text of the amendment itself, especially its phrase "the right of the people" may be considered indicative. See also similar use of the phrase "the people" in First, Fourth, Ninth and Tenth Amendments.

---

[1] Paglia, Camile. "The Million Mom March: What a Crock!" Salon.com, 17 May 2000.
[2] Malcom, Joyce Lee. *To Keep and Bear Arms*. Harvard University Press, 1994. Halbrook, Stephen. *That Every Man be Armed*. The Independent Institute, 1994.

The passionate and brilliant writings and speeches collected in *The Federalist Papers*, *The Anti-Federalist Papers* and *The Debate on the Constitution*, establish beyond a shadow of a doubt that the right of the individual American to keep and bear arms was one of the most important guarantees brought forth in favor of the plan to consolidate the American Republic.[3] At least eight of the original thirteen states had provisions in their constitutions that included recognition of the right of private citizens to keep and bear arms. The words of the early leaders of America eloquently expressed their view that an armed populace is: 1) a natural check against tyranny, 2) the first line of defense against enemy attack, and 3) a natural force for the right ordering of society. The founders well understood the liberties acknowledged by the Bill of Rights could only be held by a citizenry willing and able to protect its freedom, by force if necessary, from those who would attempt to seize it. The Second Amendment is Liberty's Teeth.

TYRANNY: MERELY AN ANTIQUATED EIGHTEENTH CENTURY CONCERN?

In 1787 Noah Webster wrote,

> Before a standing army can rule, the people must be disarmed; as they are in almost every kingdom of Europe. The supreme power in America cannot enforce unjust laws by the sword; because the whole body of the people are armed, and constitute a force superior to any bands of regular troops that can be, on any pretense, raised in the United States.[4]

---

[3] See *The Federalist Papers*, edited by Clinton Rossiter, Penguin Books, *The Anti-Federalist Papers* and the *Constitutional Convention Debates*, edited by Ralph Ketcham, Penguin Books, and *The Debate on the Constitution*, (two volumes) edited by Bernard Bailyn, The Library of America.
[4] *A Citizen of America*, Philadelphia October 17, 1787, quoted in *The Debate on the Constitution*, Part 1, p. 155.

When Bill Clinton was sworn into office for his first term, he warmly remembered his former professor at Georgetown University, Carroll Quigley. Aside from being the recipient of such a singular honor, Quigley may have helped shape some of the attitudes toward the Second Amendment held by the most anti-gun president in American history. Quigley wrote in his 1966 tome *Tragedy and Hope*,

> In a period of specialist weapons the minority who have such weapons can usually force the majority who lack them to obey; thus a period of specialist weapons tends to give rise to a period of minority rule and authoritarian government. But a period of amateur weapons is a period in which all men are roughly equal in military power, a majority can compel a minority to yield, and majority rule or even democratic government tends to rise...[6]

At the present time, there seems to be little reason to doubt that the specialist weapons of today will continue to dominate the military picture into the foreseeable future. If so, there is little reason to doubt that authoritarian rather than democratic political regimes will dominate the world into the same foreseeable future.[7]

Undeterred by this nightmarish conclusion, Quigley quickly displays the confidence in alternate solutions and concern for the "quality of life" that undoubtedly touched the heart of his young protege;

A period that is not democratic in its political structure is not necessarily bad, and may well be one in which people can live a rich and full social or intellectual life whose value may be even more significant than a democratic political or military structure.[8]

---

[6] Quigley, Carroll. *Tragedy and Hope*. Macmillan, 1966, p. 34.
[7] *Ibid.*, pp. 1200-1201.
[8] *Ibid.*, p. 1201.

OVERTURNING THE CONSTITUTION

The civilian disarmament movement is working relentlessly to avoid the one legal means of enacting gun control- namely to amend the Constitution to either repeal the Second Amendment or to legally modify it. No lovers of the limitations on government imposed by the Constitution, gun control zealots are well aware of the obstacles placed in the path of "reformers" who seek to change it. A two-thirds majority of Congress may propose amendments which must then be adopted by three-fourths of the states. Even with these protections, such idiotic amendments as Prohibition will occur. However, this is not the concern of the civilian disarmament crowd who seek to bypass the Constitution altogether.

As Jaime Sneider wrote,

> [T]he language of organizers and supporters of the Million Mom March hints at a growing trend that culminated in yesterday's March. The (generally left-leaning) disgruntled individuals who have failed politically in getting gun control measures passed have come to support Constitutional Nullification... Perhaps the scariest thing about the gun control movement is that they want to blur the existence of truth itself. According to their own words, gun-control leaders will not stop until the private ownership of guns is illegal and the Constitution overthrown. As such, they encourage nullification of the universal moral truths contained within that document. As the gun control activists pursue their agenda by any means necessary, supporting ever larger and more intrusive government, the true ethical purpose of the Second Amendment will only become more apparent.[9]

---

9 Sneider, Jaime. "Taking Aim at the Constitution:' Columbia Daily Spectator as reported by National Review, 15 May 2000.

The following news report is especially instructive in that regard.

> United Nations Secretary-General Kofi Annan has called on the international community to stem the proliferation of small arms across the world. He told a special meeting of the Security Council that restricting the flow of such weapons would be a key challenge in preventing conflict in the next century. Estimates of the number of firearms in the world range from 100 million to 500 million. Mr. Annan said there was 'no single tool of conflict so widespread, so easily available, and so difficult to restrict, as small arms' ... In his report Mr. Annan recommended that member states should: 'Adopt gun control laws including a prohibition of unrestricted trade and private ownership of small arms.'[10] [emphasis added]

---

[10] BBC Online News Network, 25 September 1999.

This is nothing less than an open call to overturn the U.S. Constitution and the Second Amendment in favor of "international law"–the infamous New World Order.

GUN CONTROL AND AMERICAN CULTURE

On the day of the march, an estimated 20,000 U.S. gun laws were on the books. To quote Ms. Paglia again,

> The Million Moms would do much more for this country if they would focus on the breakdown of family and community ties that produce sociopaths like the goons who shoot up schools and day care centers. It was parental irresponsibility and neglect, and not simply the availability of guns, that were ultimately at the root of the Columbine massacre, where home-barbecue propane tanks had been converted into bombs.

	Non-Gun Owners (Adolescent Grp.)	Illegal Gun Owners	Legal Gun Owners
Street Crimes	24%	74%	14%
Gun Crimes	1%	24%	0%

The Moms might also have consulted the 1994 report of the rabidly anti-gun Janet Reno-led Justice Department, *Urban Delinquency and Substance Abuse: Initial Findings Research Summary*[11] (see Table). Boys who own legal firearms were found to have the lowest rate of compared to both those owning illegal guns, and those owning none.

The study attributed the disparity in part to the "socialization into gun ownership," of boys with their fathers who owned guns for hunting and sport. One might suppose the close parental bonding would be equally salutary for young girl shooters as well.

---

[11] Discussed by Robert W. Lee in *The New American*, 24, April 2000.

CREATING PUBLIC OPINION

The American public is fed a daily dose of cooked statistics reminiscent of George Orwell's novel 1984. However, the tragic consequences of this propaganda on national policy threaten real life and real people. The general willingness of the American population to believe the lies of politicians and media spin-masters, and the lack of interest in alternative news sources, are disturbing. An informed electorate can make decisions. A brainwashed mass merely regurgitates its conditioning.

Geoffrey Dickens, Senior Analyst of the respected Media Research Center, detailed his group's two-year study of the treatment of gun related issues by four evening news shows (ABC's World News Tonight, the CBS Evening News, CNN's The World Today, and NBC's Nightly News) and three morning broadcasts (ABC's Good Morning America, CBS's This Morning, and NBC's Today). The study tracked these shows from July 1, 1997 to June 30, 1999.[12]

The criteria for categorization of stories as either "anti-gun" or "pro-gun" were the following: anti-gun statements were defined as ideas like "violent crimes occur because of guns;" and "gun control prevents crime;" pro-gun statements included ideas such as "criminals, not guns, cause crime," "Americans have a constitutional right to keep and bear arms," and "Concealed carry laws help reduce crime." If such statements in a news reports were weighted in a ratio of 1.5:1, the story or segment was identified as either anti-gun or pro-gun. If the ratio was less than 1.5:1, the story was regarded as neutral.

---

[12] Dickens, Geoffrey. "Outgunned: How the Network News Media are Spinning the Gun Control Debate:' *The American Rifleman*, April 2000.

In 653 gun policy stories, the study found stories advocating more gun control outnumbered stories opposing gun control by 357 to 36–a ratio of nearly 10:1 (with 260 categorized as neutral). Anti-gun sound bites were twice as frequent as those with a pro-gun message, 412 to 209. Gun control advocates appeared on morning shows 82 times compared with 37 gun rights advocates and 58 neutral spokesmen. There were 300 evening news segments which rated as follows: 164 anti-gun, 20 pro-gun, and 116 neutral. Talking heads were gun control advocates by a 2:1 ratio. Of 353 gun policy segments on morning news shows, anti-gun stories outnumbered pro-gun by 193 to 15 or a ratio of 13:1 (with 145 categorized as neutral).

A FAMILIAR HALF-DOZEN ANTI-GUN LIES

1. The "Dead Children" Lie

In the words of David Kopel, "A full listing of the lies told by the antigun lobby could fill a book."[13] Perhaps the most egregious of such is the Myth of the Dead Children. How many days go by each week when some government hack or media news reader doesn't bow his or her head and solemnly intone the quantitative figures of children killed every day by guns. Our minds are forced to conjure images of more than a hundred children a week lying dead like little well-fed Biafrans in front of Daddy's bloody night stand.

In truth, the per-capita number of fatal gun accidents among children is at its lowest level since 1903, when statistics started being kept. Furthermore, the actual number of

---

[13] Kopel, David, Research Director of the Independence Institute. "An Army of Gun Lies:' *National Review*, 17 April 2000.

child firearm fatalities is also declining every year, even as the numbers of people with firearms in their homes increases. By way of example, in 1995, there were 1,400 accidental firearm deaths in America of which 30 involved children four and younger, while 170 involved the five- to fourteen-year-old age bracket (thus 200 children in total). By comparison 2,900 children died in motor vehicles, 950 died by drowning, and 1,000 died by fire and burns. *More children die in bicycle accidents each year than by firearms*[14]. Nobody wants even one child to die. Reducing firearm accidents even further is the goal of the NRA's brilliant Eddie Eagle Program, a common sense and effective firearm safety educational effort for children—which has been boycotted, ignored, and slandered by the gun banners.

The mournful statistical mantra of the mass media/ civilian disarmament lobby are cynically based on counting young adults as children. Thus a teenage gangland slaying, a young fleeing felon shot by a police officer, a jealous twenty-one year-old shooting his wife's seducer in a bar, or a crack deal gone bad, are all counted as "children who die by firearms." Accidents are a part of life and cannot be regulated away. But the shamelessness with which these statistics are manipulated to provide fodder for those seeking to expand the range of government control is important to note.

2. *The "Guns Cause Crime" Lie*

"Normal" people do not turn into crazed maniacs when a gun is placed in their hands any more than guns levitate from tables, pockets, or closets to discharge themselves and kill

---

[14] Lott, John Jr. *More Guns, Less Crime*. University of Chicago Press, 1998, p. 9.

innocent people. The oft-repeated statement that a gun in the home is 43 times more likely to kill a family member than a criminal is another purposeful distortion of the truth to serve a political agenda. "Of the 43 deaths, 37 are suicides; and while there are obviously many ways in which a person can commit suicide, only a gun allows a small woman a realistic opportunity to defend herself at a distance from a large male predator.[15] Another of the big lies of the gun control lobby is that most people are killed by people they know. This argument is concocted from the FBI Uniform Crime Report which states that family murders account for 18 percent of murders, while 40 percent were those who "knew" their victims. The category of "those who knew their victim" however includes drug dealers and buyers, prostitutes and clients, cab drivers killed by passengers, rival gang members involved in turf wars, and murderous barroom brawlers.

Perhaps a more telling statistic is that in 1988, more than 89 percent of adult murderers had adult criminal records.[16] To put it in even simpler terms-bad people do bad things.

John Lott's monumental study of gun ownership in the United States covered all 3,054 U.S. counties from 1977 to 1992, supplemented with data for 1993 and 1994. He reached the following conclusion, "Of all the methods studied so far by economists, the carrying of concealed handguns appears to be the most cost-effective method for reducing crime.[17] The positive effect of reducing violent crime is particularly

---

[15] Kopel, David, "*An Army of Gun Lies.*" *National Review*, 17 April 2000.

[16] Lott, John Jr. *More Guns, Less Crime*. University of Chicago Press, 1988.

[17] *Ibid.*, p. 20.

significant for women who carry guns[18]. Furthermore, misuse of firearms by the millions of American carry permit holders has proven to be virtually nil. It appears *hoplophobic*[20] journalists may be more susceptible to road rage fantasies than real gun owners are.

3. The "Guns are Dangerous to Their Owners" Lie

Professor Lott quotes surveys that indicate ninety-eight percent of the time people use guns defensively, they merely need to brandish them before a criminal to stop the inevitable attack. According to Lott, fifteen national polls, including those conducted by The Los Angeles Times and Gallup, record between 760,000 and 3.5 million defensive uses of guns per year. Florida State University Department of Criminology Professor Gary Kleck conducted a survey in 1993 which found 2.5 million crimes are thwarted each year by gun-owning Americans. His National Self-Defense Survey excluded cases where people picked up a gun to investigate

---

[18] As this article was being completed, the annual Puerto Rican Day Parade took place in New York City on June 11, 2000. Following the event more than 50 women filed complaints of sexual assault against some 60 men. Allegations that police stood idly by as the attacks took place rocked the media and led New York's then-Mayor Rudy Giuliani to proclaim that heads would roll. Imagine if just one of those women had been properly armed. Sixty drunken misogynists would have run like rabbits. Such an outrage is most unlikely to occur in the 31 of 50 states that enjoy "shall issue" concealed weapons permit laws.

[19] "I coined the term *hoplophobia*... in the sincere belief that we should recognize a very peculiar sociological attitude for what it is–a more or less hysterical neurosis rather than a legitimate political position. It follows convention in the use of Greek roots in describing specific mental afflictions. *Hoplon* is the Greek word for 'instrument; but refers synonymously to 'weapon' since the earliest and principal instruments were weapons. Phobos is Greek for 'terror' and medically denotes unreasoning panic rather than normal fear. Thus hoplophobia is a mental disturbance characterized by irrational aversion to weapons, as opposed to justified apprehension about those who may wield them:' (Quote from Cooper, Jeff. *To Ride, Shoot Straight, and Speak the Truth*. Wisdom Publishing, p. 16.)

suspicious noises and the like, and focused on actual confrontations between the intended victim and the offender.[20]

4. The "Success of the Brady Law" Lie

That the Clinton/Gore Administration boasted half a million people have been stopped by Brady Law background checks creates an interesting case of cognitive dissonance. Like those amazing body counts reported by the press during the Vietnam War, that if added together would have accounted for the population of India, there seems an inherent mathematical flaw. If half a million people committed the felony of illegally attempting to purchase a weapon when they were already legally banned from such actions by Federal law, why have there been merely a dozen arrests?[21]

5. The "Gun Show Loophole" Lie

The dreaded Gun Show loophole fretted over by the media and civilian disarmament proponents is a complete sham. If a person is engaged in gun dealing for profitable purposes, they need to have a Federal Firearms License to do so or they are committing a felony. If an FPL dealer sells a firearm at a gun show, the exact same laws apply as if they sold it out a store or home. In other words, identification provided by the buyer, Form 4473 filled out, a background check, and complete record keeping including make model and serial number of the weapon purchased.

---

[20] LaPierre, Wayne. *Guns, Crime and Freedom*. Regnery Publishing, 1994, p. 23.
[21] According to the statistics quoted by Wayne LaPierre in the April 2000 official NRA publication, *The American Rifleman*.

Question: What is the famous "Gun Show Loophole?"
Answer: Private sales that take place at Gun Shows.

In other words, as a gun owner I might want to trade up to a new rifle. Knowing a gun show was to be in town, I might put a little flag in the barrel of my old rifle with a "For Sale" written on it. I would have my gun checked by the police at the door, a trigger lock put on it, and hopefully find someone else looking for a bargain. After examining and recording each other's driver's licenses to verify it was an in-state sale and therefore not in violation of the 1968 Gun Control Act, and asking my buyer if he or she is a felon (and determining to the best of my ability that he is not), and therefore not subjecting myself to a ten-year prison sentence for selling to a felon, fugitive or drug user, we would conclude the transaction. Alternately, if I died and my wife wanted to raise some cash to bury my dead ass, she might take a couple of my guns to a gun show, rent a table, and try to sell them for a decent price. If she was earning a living from this, she would be a felon. However, if she was truly making private sales it would be legal in most states.

What the civilian disarmament lobby wants to do is make sure every gun is registered, and every transfer is recorded. That way, when they achieve the power to round up guns in private hands, they'll have everyone's address and know exactly what everyone owns. One of their key sophistries is that since cars are registered, why not register guns? However, unlike cars, boats or airplanes, the possession of firearms is specifically enumerated as a right of *the people*-a right protected from infringement by the same Government that registers cars.

6. The "Other Countries Have Better Gun Laws" Lie

To begin, I agree with Camille Paglia's sentiment, Neither do crime statistics from other countries carry much weight with me. Only the U.S. has a complex Bill of Rights with a First Amendment guaranteeing 'freedom of speech' and a Second Amendment guaranteeing 'the right of the people to keep and bear arms' which remain our protection against government tyranny. It's no coincidence that this most heavily armed nation in the world is also the most individualistic and entrepreneurial, with incandescent creativity in the high-tech field that has transformed the economy.

Other English-speaking countries have not improved their societies as much as the major news organizations would like us to believe. Dr. Miquel Faria Jr. informs us that the Australian crime rate is increasing exponentially following their infamous 1996 gun ban. In 1998, the first year after implementation of the ban, the Australian crime rate experienced a 44 percent increase in armed robberies, an 8.6 percent increase in aggravated assault, and a 3.2 percent increase in homicides. In the state of Victoria, there was a 300 percent increase in the number of homicides committed with a firearm. In South Australia, robberies increased by nearly 60 percent. In 1999, armed robberies in Australia were up 73 percent, unarmed robberies increased by 28 percent, kidnappings 38 percent, assaults by 17 percent, and manslaughter by 29 percent. During the previous 25 years before banning firearms, Australia enjoyed a steady decrease in the rate of both homicides with firearms and armed robbery.[22]

---

[22] Faria, Miquel Jr., M.D., Editor-in-Chief of *The Medical Sentinel*, the official publication of the Association of American Physicians and Surgeons. "Gun Control in Australia-Chaos Down Under'.' *The New American*, 22 May 2000.

England has not done much better. After Britain's even more stringent gun control laws were enacted in 1996, the 1998 armed crime rate grew 10 percent throughout 1997 despite a 19 percent decrease in the number of registered firearms. *The London Sunday Times* for January 16, 2000 estimated upward of three million illegal guns circulating in Britain. In some areas, the Times estimated as many of one-third of criminals from fifteen- to twenty-five-years-old owned or have access to firearms.[23] In Canada and Britain, almost half of all burglaries take place when the occupants are at home. In the better armed United States, only 13 percent of burglaries are perpetrated by those brave or foolish enough to take that risk[24].

GUNS AND RACE

America's first state and local gun laws were nearly all designed to keep guns out of the hands of slaves. These included laws passed prior to the American Revolution. After the Civil War, nearly every American gun law sought to keep guns out of the hands of freed former slaves. Thus gun control has always had a particularly odious racial cast. However this is also true to an alarming degree of crime.

The Welfare State has failed miserably. In four decades, it has created a permanent crime-ridden under class whose family structure has been destroyed by regulations that encourage out-of-wedlock births and social and political policies that 1) pay people not to work, and 2) export unskilled labor manufacturing jobs overseas. Thus America has created an alternate inner city sub-culture that serves as both a permanent threat to social well-being, and an object lesson in collectivism. Yet it also serves to provide statistics for the civilian disarmament movement. The horrific crime rate among inner city poor allows for the assertion that guns kill

---

[23] Lee, Robert W. "English Crime Rate" *The New American*, 24 April 2000.
[24] Lott, John Jr. *More Guns, Less Crime*. University of Chicago Press, 1998, p. 5.

people who simply cannot be trusted to own a twenty-ounce mechanical device; that somehow, these objects seem to exert a mysterious force–especially on the psyche of America's racial minorities. This is the justification behind the crippling spate of lawsuits filed against the gun industry by big city mayors and the Department of Housing and Urban Development. Rather than leading a chorus of outrage against this insidious racial insult, the left-wing National Association for the Advancement of Colored People (NAACP) has threatened its own lawsuit against the gun industry because of the "disproportionate" effect of gun violence in the black community.

On the other hand, there is an appalling amount of black crime. According to Department of Justice figures compiled for 1997, the incidence of black crime is proportionately far greater than white. A reasonable similarity appears to exist between crime figures and arrest figures. For example, according to the Department of Justice survey for 1997, 60 percent of robberies were reported to have been committed by blacks, while 57 percent of those arrested for robberies were black.[25] The FBI Uniform Crime Report for 1992 found 55 percent of those arrested for murder were black, while 43.4 percent of murder victims were also black. The FBI found that in 1992, 94 percent of black victims were slain by black assailants[26]. Thus, when gun control advocates talk of banning "cheap handguns;' the result of their efforts, if successful, will be to leave poor people in high crime areas defenseless. Ironically, it seems modern efforts at gun control are as unconscionably racist as earlier gun control policies.[27]

---

[25] Taylor, Jared. "What Color is Crime?" *The Resister*, Vol. 5, No. 3, Summer/Autumn 1999.
[26] Bolton, John. "Counter-Propaganda 101:' *The Resister*, Vol. 4, No. 2, Winter 1998.
[27] Conversely, the Department of Justice figures for interracial crime in 1994 report that 89 percent of single offender crimes and 94 percent of multiple offender crimes were committed by blacks against whites. If these figures are rendered as violent crime per 100,000, 3,494 blacks out of 100,000 committed a violent crime against a white person in 1994, while 64 whites out of a 100,000 committed a violent crime against a black person. (Statistics from Taylor, Jared. "What Color is Crime?" *The Resister*, Vol. 5, No. 3, Summer/Autumn 1999.)

As a law-abiding American citizen who lives in a normal environment, I refuse to be treated like some seventeen-year-old, out of control, inner city gang banger, hopped up on crack, and suffering from a dearth of moral values. My children and I were raised to exhibit both the respect for life and personal self-control required to enjoy the freedom to keep and bear arms.

ALARMING PRECEDENTS FOR NATIONAL GUN REGISTRATION

From 1789 to 1934 there was not one federal gun law-with the exception of the Second Amendment. The first unconstitutional gun law was passed as the 1934 National Firearms Act which sought to ban automatic weapons by burdening them with heavy taxes and unprecedented registration requirements. The next one was the 1968 Gun Control Act, modeled nearly word for word after gun laws enacted by the Nazi regime.

The Nazis inherited the German 1928 Law on Firearms and Ammunition which required registration and renewable permits for firearm owners and their firearms, mandated permits for the acquisitions of ammunition, and the issuance of hunting permits. All firearms had to be stamped with serial numbers and the names of their manufacturers. When the Nazis came to power in 1933, they thus had access to the name and home address of every legal gun owner in Germany, along with a description of their weapons.

The Nazi Weapons Law of 1938 guaranteed only friends of the Nazi Party could own and carry firearms. Jews of course were forbidden to own guns or to participate in any business dealing in weapons. Carry permits were required in order to bear arms and were only issued to "persons of undoubted reliability, and only if a demonstration of need is set forth.

In *Gun Control: Gateway to Tyranny*, Jay Simpkin and Aaron Zelman lay out the 1938 Nazi Weapons Law with a paragraph by paragraph comparison to the U.S. Gun Control Act of 1968.[29] Anyone interested in seeking the basis for U.S. gun control legislation is recommended to make this fearless comparison. The authors also present documentary evidence that Senator Thomas Dodd (D-CT), one of the authors of the 1968 law, had several months earlier submitted official requests to the Library of Congress for an English translation of the 1938 Nazi Weapons Law.

GUN CONTROL DOES WORK TO ACCOMPLISH THE WRONG RESULTS

Gun Control is a successful mechanism for the establishment of tyranny. Between 75 and 86 million Americans own between 200 million and 240 million guns[30]. Who is going to check that each one of these guns is properly registered by each of these gun owners? Who is going to come into your house to insure a gun lock is installed on your weapon? Do you want your neighbor encouraged to inspect your home to determine how you store your gun before allowing their children to play with yours? Should your kids be programmed to report your guns to the D.A.R.E officer in their schools? Given the nature of people, if all guns mysteriously disappeared into thin air, would the rates of murder, assault and suicide really decline?

---

[29] Simpkin, Jay and Zelma, Aaron, both of Jews For the Preservation of Firearm Ownership. "Gun Control: Gateway to Tyranny;' 1993.
[30] Lott, John Jr. *More Guns, Less Crime*. University of Chicago Press, 1998.

Pop Quiz: Was the War on Drugs more effective in: a) limiting the manufacture, availability, and use of drugs, or b) filling our nations prisons while extending the powers of the Police State?

My advice to any reader who still values his or her freedom, and continues to assert the sacred right of self-preservation, is to make the effort to familiarize yourself with guns. Take the time and training required to learn to use a gun well. Once you are comfortable enough to make a choice, buy a good one and practice with it. Join the NRA immediately and contribute regularly. Speak to your friends, family and neighbors.

Make phone calls and send letters to politicians. Remind them you intend to hold their feet to the fire of the Constitution. No matter how many people tell you otherwise, the Constitution is still the law of the land. Consider the next time you hear some media sycophant drooling about the "international community" that our freedoms are unique to America. Each one of us had better be an active advocate of Liberty-otherwise, Liberty will vanish.

William S. Burroughs describes the title of his novel *Naked Lunch* as "a frozen moment when everyone sees what is on the end of every fork." I therefore make the following recommendation to anyone who plans to vote for any politician who endorses gun control. First, burn a copy of the Bill of Rights. Then pull the lever to cast your vote. That way, at least you can say you had the courage to acknowledge the future you were creating.

JANUARY 13, 2011:

Just as this book was going to press, a mass shooting occurred in Tucson, Arizona in which a Democrat House member was severely wounded, and a Republican judge and young girl killed along with several others. A mad man was responsible and a photo of him basking in his media notoriety was soon broadcast worldwide. Even faster than the release of the photo, however-within just two hours of the shooting-a Nobel prize-winning moron from *The New York Times* blamed talk radio and the Tea Party.

Later that day, a half-witted Arizona county sheriff attempted to cover his tracks by blaming those who rejected Obama's takeover of healthcare. We then learned the murderer had made at least five death threats investigated and ignored by the sheriff's department. Statistics of the sheriff's poor crime fighting record emerged. Because law enforcement had not properly referred the perpetrator to mental health authorities, the killer was able to pass an FBI background check and purchase his weapon.

The shooting was referred to as a "tragedy." It was not a tragedy. It was an outrage, a crime, an obscenity. The tragedy was that left wing media outlets and corrupt politicians were trying to get away with blaming adult political discourse for the behavior of a lunatic. Before the blood was dry, Democrat Carolyn McCarthy was introducing anti-gun legislation so the rest of us could be as defenseless as her husband-killed on the Long Island Railroad by a black racist in 1993—or the unarmed Virginia Tech students in 2007. So tedious. Yet, we go forth on.

OSHO Bhagwan Shree Rajneesh
Enlightened Master, Teacher and One of the
Greatest Religious Leaders of All Time

REBELLION IS THE BIGGEST "YES" YET

OSHO (Bhagwan Shree Rajneesh)
Author of the New Falcon Publication title:
Rebellion, Revolution & Religiousness

Beloved Master. All the historical rebellions have a huge "no" at their source. Your rebellion of the soul is centered in the mystery of "Yes." *Will you please speak to us on the alchemy of "Yes"?*

There are a few very fundamental things to be understood.

First, there has never been a rebellion in the past, only revolutions. And the distinction between a revolution and a rebellion is so vast that unless you understand the difference you will not be able to figure the way out of the puzzle of your question. Once you understand the difference...

Revolution is a crowd, a mob phenomenon. Revolution is a struggle for power: one class of people who are in power are thrown out by the other class of people who have been oppressed, exploited to such a point that now even death does not matter. They don't have anything. Revolution is a struggle between the haves and have-nots.

I am reminded of the last statement in the Communist Manifesto by Karl Marx. It is tremendously beautiful, and with a little change I can use it for my own purposes.

First its exact statement: he says, "Proletariate"–his word for the have-nots–Proletariat of the world unite, and don't be afraid because you have nothing to lose except your chains."

Moments come in history when a small group of people–cunning, clever–start exploiting the whole society. All the money goes on gathering on one side and all the poverty and starvation on the other. Naturally this state cannot be continued forever. Sooner or later those who have nothing are going to overthrow those who have all.

Revolution is a class action, it is a class struggle. It is basically political; it has nothing to do with religion, nothing to do with spirituality. And it is also violent, because those who have power are not going to lose their vested interest easily; it is going to be a bloody, violent struggle in which thousands, sometimes millions of people will die.

Just in the Russian Revolution thirty million people were killed. The czar's whole family–he was the king of Russia before the revolution–was killed by the revolutionaries so brutally that it is inconceivable. Even a six-month-old girl was also killed. Now, she was absolutely innocent, she had done no harm to anybody; but just because she belonged to the royal family... The whole royal family had to be destroyed completely. Seventeen people were killed, and not just killed but cut into pieces.

It is bound to happen in a revolution. Centuries of anger ultimately turn into blind violence.

And the last thing to remember: revolution changes nothing. It is a wheel: one class comes into power, others become powerless. But sooner or later the powerless are going to become the majority, because the powerful don't want to share their power, they want to have it in as few hands as possible.

Now, you cannot conceive in this country... There are nine hundred million people, but half the capital of the country is just in Bombay. Nine hundred million people in the whole country, and half the capital of the whole country is just in a small city. How long can it be tolerated? Revolution comes naturally, automatically–it is sometimes blind and mechanical, part of evolution. And when the powerful become the smaller group, the majority throws them away and another power group starts doing the same.

That's why I say revolution has never changed anything, or in other words, all the revolutions of history have failed. They promised much, but nothing came out of it. Even after seventy years, in the Soviet Union people are still not getting enough nourishment. Yes, there are no more the old czars and counts and countesses and princesses and princes–but in a vast ocean of poverty, even if you remove those who have power and riches it is not going to make the society rich; it is just like trying to make the ocean sweet by dropping teaspoonfuls of sugar in it.

All that has happened is a very strange phenomenon that nobody takes notice of. Only, poverty has been distributed equally: now in the Soviet Union everybody is equally poor. But what kind of revolution is this? The hope was that everybody would be equally rich.

But just by hoping you cannot become rich. Richness needs a totally different ideology of which mankind is absolutely unaware. For centuries it has praised poverty and condemned richness, comfort, luxury. Even it the poor revolt and come into power, they don't have any idea what to do with this power, how to generate energy to create more richness, comfort and luxury for the people. Because deep down in their minds there is a guilty feeling about richness, about luxury, about comfort.

So they are in a tremendous anguish, although they have come to power. This is the moment they could change the whole structure of the society, its whole productive idea.

They could bring more technology; they could drop stupid kinds of wastage.

Every country is wasting almost ten percent of its income on the army. Even the poorest country, even this country is doing the same idiotic thing. Fifty percent of the people in this country are on the verge of any day becoming an Ethiopia, a bigger Ethiopia. In Ethiopia one thousand people were dying per day. The day India starts becoming another Ethiopia–and it is not far away–then one thousand will not do; it will be many thousands of people dying every day.

By the end of this century the population of India will be the biggest in the whole world. So far it has never been; it has always been China that was ahead. By the end of the century–and there are not many years left, just within twelve years we will be reaching the end–India will have one billion people. Five hundred million people are bound to die, because there is no food for so many people.

But still the politicians, those who are in power, are not concerned at all what happens to humanity. Their concern is whether power remains in their hands or not. The can sacrifice half of the country, but they will go on making efforts to have atomic weapons, nuclear missiles.

It is a very insane kind of society that we have created in thousands of years. Its insanity has come now to a high peak. There is no going back. It seems we are all sitting on a volcano which can explode any moment.

Revolutions in the past have happened all around the world, but no revolution has succeeded in doing what it promised. It promised equality, without understanding the psychology of human individuality. Each human individual is so unique that to force them to equality is not going to make people happy, but utterly miserable.

OSHO Bhagwan Shree, known as one of the most famous, and to some, infamous, religious leaders of modern times.

I also love the idea of equality, but in a totally different way. My idea of equality is equal opportunity for all to be unique and themselves. Certainly they will be different from each other, and a society which does not have variety and differences is a very poor society. Variety brings beauty, richness, color.

But it has not yet dawned on the millions around the world that revolution has not helped, and they still go on thinking in terms of revolution. The have not understood anything from the history of man.

It is said that history repeats itself. I say it is not history that repeats itself; it only seems to repeat itself because man is absolutely unconscious and he goes on doing the same thing again and again without learning anything, without becoming mature, alert and aware.

When all the revolutions have failed some new door should be opened. There is no point in again and again changing the powerful into the powerless and the powerless into the powerful; this is a circle that goes on moving.

I don't preach revolution.

I am utterly against revolution.

I say unto you that my word for the future, and for those who are intelligent enough in the present, is *rebellion*.

What is the difference?

Rebellion is individual action; it has nothing to do with the crowd. Rebellion has nothing to do with politics, power, violence. Rebellion has something to do with changing your consciousness, your silence, your being. It is a spiritual metamorphosis.

And each individual passing through a rebellion is not fighting with anybody else, but is fighting only with his own darkness. Swords are not needed, bombs are not needed; what is needed is more alertness, more meditativeness, more love, more prayerfulness, more gratitude. Surrounded by all these qualities you are born anew.

I teach this new man, and this rebellion can become the womb for the new man I teach. We have tried collective efforts and they have failed. Now let us try individual efforts. And if one man becomes aflame with consciousness, joy and blissfulness, he will become contagious to many more.

Rebellion is a very silent phenomenon that will go on spreading without making any noise and without even leaving any footprints behind. It will move from heart to heart in deep silences, and the day it has reached to millions of people without any bloodshed, just the understanding of those millions of people will change our old primitive animalistic ways.

It will change our greed, and the day greed is gone there is no question of accumulating money. No revolution has been able to destroy greed; those who come into power become greedy.

We have passed through a revolution just now in this

country, and it is a very significant example to understand. The people who were leading the revolution in this country against the British rule were followers of Mahatma Gandhi, who preached poverty, who preached non-possessiveness. The moment they came into power all his disciples started living in palaces which were made for viceroys. All his disciples who had been thinking their whole lives that they are servants of the people became masters of the people.

There is more corruption in this country than anywhere else. This is very strange–this is Gandhian corruption, very religious, very pious, and the people who are doing it were trained, disciplined to be servants of the people. But power has a tremendous capacity to change people; the moment you have power you are immediately a different person. You start behaving exactly like any other powerful person who have gone before.

Nothing has changed. Only the British are gone, and in their place a single party has been ruling for forty years. Now it is not just a single party, but a single family; it has become a dynasty. And the exploitation continues and the poverty continues–it has grown at least a hundred times more since the British Empire has been gone.

Everything has deteriorated–the morality, the character, the integrity, everything has become a commodity. You can purchase anybody; all you need is money. There is not a single individual in the whole country who is not a commodity in the marketplace; all you need is money. Everybody is purchasable–judges are purchasable, police commissioners are purchasable, politicians are purchasable. Even under the British rule this country has never known such corruption.

What has the country gained? The rulers have changed, but what does this signify? Unless there is a rebelliousness spreading from individual to individual, unless we can create an atmosphere of enlightenment around the world where greed will fall down on its own accord, where anger will not be possible, where violence will become impossible, where love will be just the way you live...where life should be respected, where the boy should be loved, appreciated, where comfort should not be condemned. It is natural to ask for comfort.

Even the trees... In Africa, trees grow very high; the same trees in India don't grow that high. I was puzzled, what happens? I was trying to find out why they should grow to the same height but they don't, and the reason I found was that unless there is a density of trees, trees won't grow high. Even at a lesser height the sun is available, and that is their comfort, that is their life, that is their joy. In Africa the jungles are so thick that every tree tries in every way to grow as high as possible, because only then can it have the joy of the sun, the joy of the rain, the joy of the wind. Only then can it dance; otherwise the is nothing but death.

The whole of nature wants comfort, the whole of nature wants all the luxury that is possible. But our religions have been teaching us against luxury, against comfort, against riches.

A man of enlightenment sees with clarity that is it unnatural to demand from people, "You should be content with your poverty, you should be content with your sicknesses, you should be content with all kinds of exploitation, you should be content and you should not try to rise higher, to reach to the sun and the rain and the wind." This is absolutely unnatural conditioning that we are all carrying. Only a rebellion in your being can bring you to this clarity.

You say that in history all the rebellions were based on "no." Those were not rebellions; change the word. All the revolutions were based on "no." They were negative, they were against something, they were destructive, they were revengeful and violent.

Certainly, my rebellion is based on "yes"–yes to existence, yes to nature, yes to yourself. Whatever the religions may be saying and whatever the ancient traditions may be saying, they are all saying no to yourself, no to nature, no to existence; they are all life-negative.

My rebellion is life-affirmative. I want you to dance and sing and love and live as intensely as possible and as totally as possible. In this total affirmation of life, in this absolute "yes" to nature we can bring a totally new earth and a totally new humanity into being.

The past was "no."

The future has to be "yes."

We have lived enough with the "no," we have suffered enough and there has been nothing but misery. I want people to be as joyful as birds singing in the morning, as colorful as flowers, as free as the bird on the wing with no bondages, with no conditioning, with no past–just an open future, an open sky and you can fly to the stars.

Because I am saying yes to life, all the no-sayers are against me, all over the world. My yes-saying goes against all the religions and against all the ideologies that have been forced upon man. My "yes" is my rebellion. The day you will also be able to say "yes" it will be your rebellion.

We can have rebellious people functioning together, but each will be an independent individual, not belonging to a political party or to a religious organization. Just out of freedom and out of love and out of the same beautiful "yes" we will meet. Our meeting will not be a contract, our meeting will not be in any way a surrender; our meeting will make every individual more individual. Supported by everybody else, our meeting will not take away freedom, will not enslave you; our meeting will give you more freedom, more support so that you can be stronger in your freedom. Long has been the slavery, and long has been our burden. We have become weak because of the thousands of years of darkness that have been poured on us.

The people who love to say "yes" who understand the meaning of rebellion, will not be alone; they will be individuals. But the people who are on the same path, fellow-travelers, friends, will be supporting each other in their meditativeness, in their joy, in their dance, in their music. They will become a spiritual orchestra, where so many people are playing instruments but creating one music. So many people can be together and yet they may be creating the same consciousness, the same light, the same joy, the same fragrance.

It is a long way–"no" seems to be a shortcut–that's why it has not been tried up to now. Whenever I have discussed it with people, they said, "Perhaps you are right, but when will it be possible that the whole earth will say 'yes'?"

I said, "Anyway we have been on this earth for millions of years and you have been saying 'no'–and what is your achievement? It is time. Give a chance to 'yes' too."

My feeling is that "no" is a quality of death; "yes" is the very center of life. "No" had to fail because death cannot succeed, cannot be victorious over life. If we give a chance to "yes" based in rebelliousness it is bound to become a wildfire, because everybody deep down wants it to happen. I have not found a single person in my life who does not want to live a natural, relaxed peaceful, silent life.

But that life is possible only if everybody else is also living the same kind of life.

I can understand the fear of people that individual rebellion may take a long time, but there is no problem in it.

In fact each individual who passes through this rebellious fire becomes at least for himself a bliss and an ecstasy, and there is every possibility that he will sow the seeds around him. But he has not failed; he has conquered, he has reached to the very peak of his potential. He has blossomed. There is nothing more that he can think of; the whole existence is his.

So as far as that individual is concerned the rebellion is complete. He will be able to sow seeds all around. And there is no hurry; eternity is available. Slowly, slowly more and more people will become more and more conscious, more alert. Enlightenment will become a common phenomenon.

It should not be that only in a while there is a Gautam Buddha, once in a while there is a Jesus, once in a while there is a Socrates–the names can be counted on only ten fingers. This is simply unbelievable. It is as if our garden is full of rosebushes, thousands of rosebushes, and once in a while one rosebush blossoms and gives you roses. And the remaining thousands remain without flowers?

Unless a rosebush comes to blossom it cannot dance– for what? It cannot share; it has nothing to share. It remains poor, empty, meaningless. Whether it lived or not makes no difference.

The only difference is that when it blossoms and offers its songs and its flowers and its fragrance to existence and to anybody who is willing to receive, the rosebush is fulfilled. Its life has not been just a meaningless drag; it has become a beautiful dance full of songs, a deep fulfillment that goes to the very roots.

I am not worried about time. If the concept is understood, time is available; enough time is available.

In the East we have a beautiful proverb: The man who loses the path in the morning, if he returns home by evening he should not be called lost. What does it matter? In the morning he went astray–just little adventures here and there–and by the evening he is back home. A few people may have come a little earlier; he has come a little late, but he is not necessarily poorer than those who have come earlier. It may be just vice versa: he may be more experienced because he has gone wandering so far astray. And then coming back again, falling and getting up–he is not necessarily a loser.

So time is not at all a consideration to me.

My rebellion is absolutely individual and it will spread from individual to individual. Sometime this whole planet is bound to become enlightened. Idiots may try to wait and see what happens to others, but they also finally have to join the caravan.

The very idea of enlightenment is so new, although it is not something that has not been known before. There have been enlightened people, but they never brought enlightenment as a rebellion. That is what is new about it. They became enlightened, they became contented, they became fulfilled, and a great fallacy happened and I have to point it out. Although I feel not to show any mistakes of the enlightened ones–I feel sad about it–but my responsibility is not for the dead. My responsibility is for those who are alive and for those who will be coming.

So I have to make it clear. Gautam Buddha, Mahavira, Adinatha, Lao Tzu, Kabir, all those people who became enlightened attained to tremendous beauty, to great joy, to utter ecstasy–to what I have been calling *satyam, shivam, sundram*, the truth, the godliness of the truth and the beauty of that godliness.

But because they had become enlightened they started teaching people to be contented: "Remain peaceful, remain silent." This is the fallacy. They attained contentment after a long search. It was a conclusion, not a beginning; it was the very end product of their enlightenment, but they started telling people that you can be contented right now: "Be fulfilled, be silent."

That's how they became anti-rebellious, without perhaps knowing that if a poor man remains contented with his poverty it is dangerous; if a slave remains contented with his slavery, it is dangerous.

So all the enlightened people of the past attained to great heights, about which there is no doubt. But there is a fallacy that they all perpetuated without exception. The fallacy is that they began telling people to start with that which comes in the end. The flower comes only in the end; one has to start with the roots, with the seed. And if you tell people to start with the roses, then the only way is to purchase roses of plastic. The only way to be contented without meditation is to be a hypocrite, because deep down you are angry, deep down you are furious, deep down you want to freak out, and on the surface you are showing immense peace. This peace has been like a cancer to humanity.

You can see it happening in this country more clearly than anywhere else, because this country was fortunate, blessed by more enlightened people than any other country– but unfortunately, because so many enlightened people committed the same fallacy, this country remained for twenty centuries continuously a slave.

"Hallelujah! came the response from the back.

The vicar managed to get to the end of the sermon, but at the end went up to the American and said, "Excuse me, I'm afraid in this country we like to keep a bit of decorum. We try to keep a stiff upper lip. It is the queen's own country, this is a place of God, and I frankly found your behavior rather disconcerting."

"Hey, man, I'm sorry, you are right on. I just loved the quaint way you gave us all that great shit about Moses and the Ten Commandments and I thought I would throw a few thousand greenbacks in your direction for this great thing going on here."

"Cool, man!" said the preacher.

It does not take much to find out what is deep inside. All decorum, all culture is so superficial; it will be a tremendous joy to see people in their authenticity, in their reality, without any decorum, without any make-up, just as they are. The world will be tremendously benefited if all this falseness disappears.

The alchemy of "yes" and the rebellion based on "yes" are capable of destroying all that is false, and discovering all that is real and has been covered for centuries, layer upon layer by every generation, so much that even you yourself have forgotten who you are.

If suddenly somebody wakes you up in the middle of the night and asks you, "Who are you?" you will take a little time to remember who you used to be the night before when you went to bed.

It happened that George Bernard Shaw was going to deliver a lecture some distance away from London. On the way in the train came the ticket-checker. George Bernard Shaw looked in every pocket, opened all his suitcases, but the ticket was not there. Finally, he was perspiring and the ticket-checker said, "Don't be worried, I know who you are; the whole country knows, the whole world knows. The ticket must be somewhere, you don't be worried. And even if its lost, I am here to help you get out of the station, wherever you want to get out."

George Bernard Shaw said, "Shut up! I am already in confusion and you are making me more confused. I am trying to remember where I am going! That ticket was the only thing...I am not searching for the ticket for you, idiot; I don't care about you, you can get lost. Bring me my ticket!"

The man said, "But how can I find your ticket?"

George Bernard Shaw said, "Then what am I supposed to do? Where should I get down? Because unless I know the name of the station..."

It is almost the same situation with everybody. You don't know who you are; your name is just a label that has been put upon you, it is not your being. Where are you going?–you don't have any ticket to show you where you are going to get down, and you are just hoping that somebody may push you somewhere, or maybe somewhere the terminus comes and the train stops and it does not go anywhere else... Just hoping.

But why are you traveling in the first place? In fact, for all those fundamental questions you have only one answer: I don't know. In this state of unawareness your revolutions cannot succeed. In this state of unawareness, your desire for freedom is just a dream. You cannot understand what freedom is. For whom are you asking freedom?

My idea of a rebellion based on "yes' means a rebellion based on meditation, for the first time in the history of man. And because each individual has to work upon himself, there is no question of any fight, there is no question of any organization, there is no question of any conspiracy, there is no question of planting bombs and hijacking airplanes.

I am not interested in hijacking airplanes, neither am I interested in destroying any governments. But it will be the final result of my individual rebellion based on meditation: government will disappear. They have to disappear; they have been nothing by a nuisance on the earth. Nations have to disappear. There is no need of any nations; the whole earth belongs to the whole of humanity. There is no need of any passports, there is no need of any visas.

This earth is ours, and what kind of freedom is there if we cannot even move? Everywhere there are barriers, every nation is a big imprisonment. Just because you cannot see the boundaries you think you are free. Just try to pass through the boundary and immediately you will be faced with a loaded gun: "Go back inside the prison. You belong in prison. You cannot enter into another prison without permission." These are your nations!

Certainly, a rebellion of my vision will take away all this garbage of nations, and discrimination between white and black, and give the whole of humanity a natural, relaxed, comfortable life. This is possible, because science has given us everything that we need, even if the population of the earth is three times more than it is today.

Just a little intelligence is needed–which will be released by meditation–and we can have a beautiful earth with beautiful people, and a multidimensional freedom which is not just a word in the dead constitution books but a living reality.

One thing finally to be remembered: the days of revolution are past. We have tried them many times, and every time the same story is repeated. Enough. Now something new is urgently needed. And except for the idea that I am giving you of a rebellion, individual and based on meditativeness, there is no other alternative proposed anywhere in the world.

And I am not a philosopher; I am absolutely pragmatic and practical. I am not only talking about meditative rebellion, I am preparing people for it. Whether you know it or not doesn't matter. Whoever comes close to me is going to become a rebellious individual, and wherever he will go he will spread this contagious health. It will make people aware of their dignity, it will make people aware of their potentiality. It will make people alert to what they can become, what they are, and why they are stuck.

My sannyasins' function is not to be missionaries, but to be so loving, compassionate, such fragrant individuals... It is not a question of converting people from one ideology to another ideology. It is a far deeper transformation–from the whole past to a totally new and unknown future. It is the greatest adventure that one can think of.

Satyam-Shivam-Sundram, Session 26, Nov. 19, 1987

Timothy Leary, Ph.D.
World famous Psychologist, Writer and Philosopher

The authors divide the stages of human history into: tribal, feudal, industrial, and cybernetic. The arrival of the latter stage is heralded in the authors' book *Cybernetic Societies*.

TWENTY-TWO ALTERNATIVES TO INVOLUNTARY DEATH

Timothy Leary, Ph.D. & Eric Gullichsen

Author of the New Falcon Publication title:
What Does WoMan Want?
The Intelligence Agents
The Game of Life
Info-Psychology
Neuropolitique

"*Death is the ultimate negative patient health outcome.*"
–William L. Roper, Director, Health Care Financing Administration (HCFA), which administers Medicare

Most human beings face death with an "attitude" of helplessness, either resigned or fearful. Neither of these submissive, often uninformed, "angles of approach" to the most crucial event of one's life can be ennobling.

Today, there are many practical options available for dealing with dying process. Passivity, failure to learn about them, might be the ultimate irretrievable blunder. Pascal's famous no-lose wager about the existence of God translates into modern life as a no-risk gamble on the prowess of technology.

For millennia the fear of death has depreciated individual confidence and increased dependence on authority.

True, the loyal member of a familial or racial gene-pool can take pride in the successes and survival tenacity of their kinship. But for the individual, the traditional prospects are less than exalted. Let's be laser-honest here. How can you be proud of your past achievements, walk tall in the present or zap enthusiastically into the future if, awaiting you implacably around some future corner, is Old Mr. D., The Grim Reaper?

What a PR job the Word Makers did to build this Death Concept into a Prime-Time Horror Show! The grave. Mortification. Extinction. Breakdown. Catastrophe. Doom. Finish. Fatality. Malignancy. Necrology. Obituary. The end.

Note the calculated negativity. To die is to croak, to give up the ghost, to bite the dust, to kick the bucket, to perish. To become inanimate, lifeless, defunct, extinct, moribund, cadaverous, necrotic. A corpse, a stiff, a cadaver, a relic, food for worms, a *corpus delicti*, a carcass. What a miserable ending to the game of life!

Fear Of Death Was An Evolutionary Necessity In The Past

In the past, the reflexive genetic duty of TOP MANAGEMENT (those in social control of the various gene-pools) has been to make humans feel weak, helpless, and dependent in the face of death. The good of the race or nation was ensured at the cost of the sacrifice of the individual.

Obedience and submission was rewarded on a time-payment plan. For his/her devotion the individual was promised immortality in the post-mortem hive-center variously known as "heaven," "paradise," or the "Kingdom of the Lord." In order to maintain the attitude of dedication, the gene-pool managers had to control the "dying reflexes," orchestrate the trigger-stimuli that activate the "death circuits" of the brain. This was accomplished through rituals that imprint dependence and docility when the "dying alarm bells" go off in the brain.

Perhaps we can better understand this imprinting mechanism by considering another set of "rituals," those by which human hives manage the conception-reproduction reflexes. A discussion of these is less likely to alarm you. And the mechanisms of control imposed by the operation of social machinery are similar in the two cases. We invite you to "step outside the system" for a moment, to vividly see what is ordinarily invisible because it is so entrenched in our expectation.

At adolescence each kinship group provides rituals, taboos, ethical prescriptions to guide the all-important sperm-egg situation.

Management by the individual of the horny DNA machinery is always a threat to hive inbreeding. Dress, grooming, dating, courtship, contraception, and abortion patterns are fanatically conventionalized in tribal and feudal societies. Personal innovation is sternly condemned and ostracized. Industrial democracies vary in the sexual freedom allowed individuals. But in totalitarian states, China and Iran for example, rigid prudish morality controls the mating reflexes and governs boy-girl relations. Under the Chinese dictator Mao, "romance" was forbidden because it weakened dedication to the state, i.e., the local gene-pool. If teenagers pilot and select their own mating, then they will be more likely to fertilize outside the hive, more likely to insist on directing their own lives, and, worst of all, less likely to rear their offspring with blind gene-pool loyalty.

Even more rigid social-imprinting rituals guard the "dying reflexes." Hive control of "death" responses is taken for granted in all pre-cybernetic societies.

In the past this conservative degradation of individuality was an evolutionary virtue.

During epochs of species stability, when the tribal, feudal and industrial technologies were being mastered and fine-tuned, wisdom was centered in the gene-pool stored in the collective linguistic-consciousness, the racial data-base of the hive.

Since individual life was short, brutish, aimless, what a singular learned was nearly irrelevant. The world was changing so slowly that knowledge could only be embodied in the species. Lacking the technologies for the personal mastery of transmission and storage of information, the individual was simply too slow, too small, to matter. Loyalty to the racial collective was the virtue. Creativity, Premature Individuation, was anti-evolutionary. A weirdo, mutant distraction. Only Village Idiots would try to commit independent, unauthorized thought.

In the feudal and industrial eras, Management used the fear of death to motivate and control individuals. Today, politicians use the death-dealing military and the police and capital punishment to protect the social order. Organized religion maintains its power and wealth by orchestrating and exaggerating the fear of death.

Among the many things that the Pope, the Ayatollah, and Fundamentalist Protestants agree on: confident understanding and self-directed mastery of the dying process is the last thing to be allowed to the individual. The very notion of *Cybernetic Post-Biological Intelligence* or consumer immortality-options is taboo, sinful. For formerly valid reasons of gene-pool protection.

Religions have cleverly monopolized the rituals of dying to increase control over the superstitious. Throughout history the priests and mullahs have swarmed around the expiring human like black vultures. Death belonging to them.

As we grow in the 20th century we are systematically programmed about How to Die. Hospitals are staffed with priests/ministers/rabbis ready to perform the "last rites."

Every army unit has its Catholic Chaplin to administer the Sacrament of Extreme Unction (what a phrase, really!) to the expiring solider. The Ayatollah, Chief Mullah of the Islamic Death Cult, sends his teenage soldiers into the Iraq mine fields with dog-tags guaranteeing immediate transfer to the Allah's Destination Resort. Koranic Heaven. A terrible auto crash? Call the medics! Call the priest! Call the Reverend!

In the Industrial Society, everything becomes part of Big Business. Dying involves Blue Cross, Medicare, Health Care Delivery Systems, the Health Care Financing Administration (HCFA), terminal patient wards. Undertakers. Cemeteries. The funeral rituals.

The monopolies of religion and the assembly lines of Top Management process dying and the dead even more efficiently than the living.

We recall that knowledge and selective choice about such gene-pool issues as conception, test-tube fertilization, pregnancy, abortion is dangerous enough to the church-fathers.

But suicide, right-to-die concepts, euthanasia, life extension, out-of-body-experiences, occult experimentation, astral-travel scenarios, death/rebirth reports, extraterrestrial speculation, cryogenics, sperm-banks, egg-banks, DNA banks, personally-empowering Artificial Intelligence Technology–anything that encourages the individual to engage in personal speculation and experimentation with immortality– is anathema to the orthodox Seed-Shepherds of the feudal and industrial ages.

Why? Because if the flock doesn't fear death, then the grip of Religious and Political Management is broken. The power of the gene-pool is threatened. And when control looses in the gene-pool, dangerous genetic innovations and mutational visions tend to emerge.

Some believe that the Cybernetic Age we are entering could mark the beginning of a period of enlightened and intelligent individualism, a time unique in history when technology is available to individuals to support a huge diversity of personalized lifestyles and cultures, a world of diverse, interacting social groups whose initial-founding membership number is one.

The exploding technology of computation and communication lays a delicious feast of knowledge and personal choice within our easy grasp. Under such conditions, the operating wisdom and control naturally passes from aeons-old power of gene pools, and locates in the rapidly self-modifying brains of individuals capable of dealing with an ever-accelerating rate of change.

Aided by customized, personally-programmed quantum-linguistic appliances, the individual can choose his/her own social genetic future. And perhaps choose not to "die."

The Wave Theory Of Evolution

Current theories of genetics suggest that evolution, like everything else in the universe, comes in waves.

So, at times of Punctuated Evolution, collective metamorphosis, when many things are mutating at the same time, then the ten commandments of the "old ones" become ten more suggestions...

At such times of rapid innovation and collective mutation, conservative hive dogma can be dangerous, suicidal. Individual experimentation and exploration, the thoughtful methodical scientific challenging of taboos, becomes the key to the survival of the gene-school.

Now, as we enter the Cybernetic Age, we arrive at a new wisdom which broadens our definition of personal immortality and gene-pool survival: *The Post-Biological Options Of The Information Species.* A fascinating set of gourmet-consumer choices suddenly appear on the pop-up menu of The Evolutionary Café.

It is beginning to look as though in the Information Society, the individual human being can script, produce, direct his/her own immortality.

Here we face Mutation Shock in its most panicky form. And, as we have done in understanding earlier mutations, the first step is to develop a new language. We should not impose our values or vocabulary of the past species upon the new Cybernetic Culture.

Would you let the buzz-words of a preliterate Paleolithic cult control your life? Will you let the superstitions of a tribal-village culture (now represented by the Pope and the Ayatollah) shuffle you off the scene? Will you let the mechanical planned obsolescence tactics of the Factory Culture manage your existence?

So let us have no more pious wimp-sheep talk about death. The time has come to talk cheerfully and joke sassily about personal responsibility for managing the dying process. For starters let's de-mystify death and develop alternative metaphors for consciousness leaving the body. Let us speculate good-naturedly about post-biological options. Let's be bold about opening up a broad spectrum of Club-Med post-biological possibilities.

For starters, let's replace the word "death" with the more neutral, precise, scientific term: *Metabolic Coma.* And then let's go on to suggest that this temporary state of "coma" might be replaced by: *Auto-Metamorphosis*, a self-controlled change in bodily form, where the individual chooses to change his/her vehicle of existence without loss of consciousness.

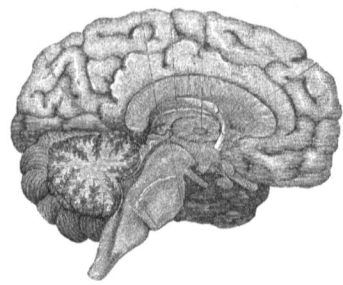 

Timothy Leary, Ph.D.,

Then, let's distinguish between involuntary and voluntary metabolic coma. Reversible and irreversible dying.

Let's explore that fascinating "no-man's land"–the period between body-death and neurological-death in terms of the knowledge-information processing involved.

And let's collect some data about that even more intriguing zone now beginning to be researched in the cross-disciplinary field of scientific study known as Artificial Life.[1] What knowledge-information processing capabilities can be preserved after both metabolic coma and brain cessation? What natural and artificial systems, from the growth of mineral structures to the self-reproduction of formal mathematical automata, are promising alternative candidates to biology for the support of life?

And then let us perform the ultimate act of Human Intelligence. Let's venture with calm, open-minded tolerance and

---

[1] Los Alamos, famous as the birthplace of atomic weapons, today also houses the Center for Nonlinear Studies. Several years ago the center sponsored a week long international workshop, the world's first, where scientists met to discuss the implications and craft the foundational theories of the field. The meeting was friendly, fun, and wildly transdisciplinary. Nanotechnology pioneers outlined the potential for protein engineering, and Hans Moravec of the Robotics Institute of Carnegie Mellon University presented compelling arguments that a genetic takeover was underway, our cultural artifacts now evolving past the point of symbiosis with the human species. Self-replicating structures ranging from minerals to computer viruses were demonstrated.

scientific rigor into that perennially mysterious *terra incognita* and ask the final question: What knowledge-information processing possibilities can remain after the cessation of all biological life: somatic, neurological and genetic?

How can human consciousness be supported in hardware outside of the moist envelop of graceful, attractive, pleasure-filled meat we now inhabit? How can the organic, carbon-constructed caterpillar become the silicon butterfly?

C.S. Hyatt, Ph.D. and A.K. O'Shea have suggested three stages of *Post-Biological Intelligence*:

1. *Cybernetic Recognition* of the myriad knowledge-information processing varieties involved in the many stages of dying.

2. *Cybernetic Management*, developing knowledge-information processing skills while out-of-body, out-of-brain, and beyond DNA.

3. *Cybernetic-Technological*, attaining one, or many, of the immortality options.

Post-Biological Recognition Intelligence

We recognize that the dying process, which for millennia has been blanketed by taboo and primitive superstition, has suddenly become accessible to human intelligence.

Here we experience the sudden insights that we need not "go quietly" and passively into the dark night or the neon-lit, Muzak-enhanced Disney-heaven of Christian televalgelist's crowd. We realize that the concept of involuntary, irreversible metabolic coma known as death is a feudal superstition, a marketing efficiency of industrial society. We understand that one can discover dozens of active, creative alternatives to going belly-up clutching the company logo of the Christian Cross, Blue Cross, Crescent Cross, or the eligibility cards of the Veterans Administration.

Recognition is always the beginning of the possibility for change. Once we comprehend that "death" can be defined as a problem of knowledge-information processing, solutions to this age-long "problem" can emerge. One realizes the intelligent thing to do is to try to keep one's knowledge-processing capacities around as long as possible. In bodily form. In neural form. In the silicon circuitry and magnetic storage media of today's computers. In molecular form, through the atom stacking of nanotechnology in tomorrow's computers. In cryogenic form. In the form of stored data, legend, myth. In the form of off-spring who are cybernetically trained to use *Post-Biological Intelligence*. In the form of post-biological gene pools, info-pools, advanced viral forms resident in world computer networks and cyberspace matrices of the sort described in the "sprawl novels" of William Gibson.[2]

The second step in attaining *Post-Biological Recognition Intelligence* is to shift from the passive to the active mode. Industrial age humans were trained to await docilely the onset of termination and then to turn over their body for disposal to the priests and the factory (hospital) technicians.

Our species is now developing the Cybernetic Information Skills to plan ahead, to make one's will prevail. The smart thing to do is to see dying as a change in the implementation of information-processing: to orchestrate it, manage it, anticipate and exercise the many available options.

We consider here twenty-two distinct methods of avoiding a submissive or fearful dying.[3]

---

[2] William Gibson, cyberpunk psy-fi visionary, has published *Neuromancer, Count Zero*, and *Burning Chrome*. They are recommended reading for their technically and socially plausible vision of high-tech low-life on the streets.
[3] Mystics may remark that there are also twenty-two paths in the Kabbalistic Tree of Life, associated with the twenty-two cards of the Major Arcana in the Tarot.

Post-Biological Programming Intelligence

Elsewhere the authors have defined eight levels of intelligence: biological emotional, mental-symbolic, social, aesthetic, neurological-cybernetic, genetic, atomic-nanotech. At each stage there is a recognition stage, followed by a brain-programming or brain-reprogramming stage.

In order to reprogram it is necessary to activate the circuits in the brain which mediate that particular dimension of intelligence. Once this circuit is "turned on" it is possible to re-imprint or reprogram.

Cognitive neurology suggests that the most direct way to reprogram emotional responses is to reactivate the appropriate circuits. To reprogram sexual responses it is effective to reactivate and re-experience the original teenage imprints and re-imprint new sexual responses.

The circuits of the brain which mediate the "dying" process are routinely experienced during "near-death" crises. For centuries people have reported: "My entire life flashed before my eyes as I sank for the third time."

This "near-death" experience can be "turned-on" via the relevant anesthetic drugs; ketamine, for example.

Or by learning enough about the effects of out-of-the-body drugs so one can use hypnotic techniques to activate the desired circuits without using external chemical stimuli.

We see immediately the rituals intuitively developed by religious groups are designed to induce trance states related to "dying:' The child growing up in a Catholic culture is deeply imprinted (programmed) by funeral rites. The arrival of the solemn priest to administer extreme unction becomes an access code for the *Post-Biological state*. Other cultures have different rituals for activating and then controlling (programming) the death circuits of the brain. Until recently, very few have permitted personal control or customized consumer choice.

Perhaps this discussion of the "dying circuits of the brain" is too innovative. Sometimes it is easier to understand new concepts about one's own species by referring to other species. Almost every animal species manifests "dying reflexes." Some animals leave the herd to die alone. Others stand with legs apart, stolidly postponing the last moment. Some species eject the dying organism from the social group.

To gain navigational control of one's dying processes three steps suggest themselves: 1) activate the death-reflexes imprinted by your culture, experience them... 2) trace their origins, and... 3) reprogram.

The aim is to develop a scientific model of the chain of cybernetic (knowledge-information) processes that occur as one approaches this metamorphic stage—and to intentionally develop options for taking active responsibility for these events.

Achieving Immortality

Since the dawn of human history, philosophers and theologians have speculated about immortality. Uneasy, aging kings have commanded methods for extending the life span.

A most dramatic example of this age-long impulse is ancient Egypt which produced mummification, the pyramids and manuals like the *Egyptian Book of the Dying*.

The Tibetan Book of the Dead (Buddhist) presents a masterful model of post-mortem stages and techniques for guiding the student to a state of immortality which is neurologically "real" and suggests scientific techniques for reversing the dying process.

The new field of molecular engineering is producing techniques within the framework of current consensus Western Science to implement auto-metamorphosis.

The aim of the game is to defeat death-to give the Individual mastery of this, the final stupidity.

The next section of this essay presents twenty-two methods of achieving immortality. We do not especially endorse any particular technique. Our aim is to review all options and encourage creative-courageous thinking about new possibilities.

A PRELIMINARY LIST OF IMMORTALITY OPTIONS
(To replace Involuntary Irreversible Metabolic Coma)

I. Psychological/Behavioral Training Techniques

The techniques in this category do not assist in attaining personal immortality per se, but are useful in acquiring the experience of "experimental dying;' reversible-voluntary exploration of the territory between body-coma and brain, death, sometimes called out-of-body experiences; or near-dying experiences. Others have termed these astral travel, or reincarnation memories.

1. Meditation and Hypnosis

These are the classic yogic routes to exploration of non-ordinary states of consciousness. They are well known to be labor and time intensive. For the most intelligent and comprehensive discussion of these techniques, we recommend Aleister Crowley.[4]

2. Carefully Designed Psychedelic Drug Experiences of "Dying" and Genetic (Reincarnation/Pre-Incarnation) Consciousness

---

[4] Crowley, Aleister. *Eight Lectures on Yoga*. (Divided into two parts respectively entitled, "Yoga for Yahoos" and "Yoga for Yellowbellies:') New Falcon Publications, 1991.

There is, here, no commitment to any occultist theory about biological incarnation. We refer to techniques enabling access to information and operational programs stored in the brain of the individual. In normal states of consciousness, these are subroutines operating below voluntary access.

3. Experimental Out-of-Body Experiences Using Anesthetics

John Lilly has written extensively about his experiences with small dosages of anesthetics such as ketamine[5]. It is possible that the out-of-body subjective effects of such substances are (merely) interpretations of proprioceptive disruption. Nevertheless, Lilly's reported experiences seem to indicate that information is available through these investigative routes.

4. Sensory Deprivation/Isolation Tanks

Again, Lilly has investigated this subject most comprehensively.

5. Reprogramming Exercises (Suspending the Effects of and Replacing Early "Death" Imprints Imposed by Culture)

6. Development of New Rituals to Guide the Post-Body Transition

Our cultural taboos have prohibited the development of much detailed work in this area. One of the few available sources in this area is E. J. Gold.[6]

7. Pre-Incarnation Exercises

With these, one uses the preferred altered state method (drugs, hypnosis, shamanic trance, voodoo ritual, born-again frenzies) to create future scripts for oneself.

---

[5] Walford, Roy L., M.D. *The 120 Year Diet*. Simon & Schuster, 1986. Norton, W. W. *Maximum Life Span*. New York, 1983.

[6] Gold, E. J. *American Book of the Dead*. IDHHB, 1973. See also Gold's *Creation Story Verbatim*.

8. Aesthetically-Orchestrated Voluntary "Dying"

This procedure has been called suicide, i.e., "self-murder;' by officials who wish to control the mortem process. Mr. and Mrs. Arthur Koestler, active members of the British EXIT program arranged a most dignified and graceful voluntary metabolic coma. A California group, HADDA, is placing an amendment on California ballot to permit terminal patients to plan voluntary metacom with their medical advisors.

The non-Californian can always look for an enlightened M.D., or consenting adult friends to act as guides to the Western Lands.

II. Somatic Techniques for Life Extension

Techniques to inhibit the process of aging comprise the classical approach to immortality. In the present state of science these "buy time."

9. Diet

The classic research on diet and longevity has been performed by Roy L. Walford, M.D.[7]

10. Life-Extension Drugs

These include antioxidants and others. A comprehensive reference is *Life Extension* by Sandy Shaw and Durk Pearson.

11. Exercise Regimes
12. Temperature Variation
13. Sleep Treatments (Hibernation)
14. Immunization to Counter the Aging Process

---

[7] Walford, Roy L., M.D. The 120 Year Diet. Simon & Schuster, 1986. Norton, W. W. Maximum Life Span. New York, 1983.

III. Somatic/Neural/Genetic Preservation

Techniques in this class do not ensure continuous operation of consciousness. They produce potentially reversible metabolic coma. They are alternatives for preserving the structure of tissues until a time of more advanced medical knowledge.

15. Cryogenics or Vacuum-Pack "Pickling"

Why let one's body and brain rot when that seems to imply no possibility at all for your future? Why let the carefully arranged tangle of dendritic growths in your nervous system which may be the storage site for all of your memories get eaten by fungus? Perpetual preservation of your tissues is available today at moderate cost.[8]

16. Cryonic Preservation of Neural Tissue or DNA

Those not particularly attached to their bodies can opt for preservation of the essentials: their brains together with the instructional codes capable of re-growing something genetically identical to their present bio-machinery.

IV. Bio-Genetic Methods for Life Extension

Is there any need to experience metabolic coma at all? We have mentioned ways to gain personal control of the experience, to stave it off by "conventional" longevity techniques, to avoid irreversible dissolution of the systemic substrate.

Techniques are now emerging to permit a much more vivid guarantee of personal persistence, a smooth metamorphic transformation into a different form of substrate on which the computer program of consciousness runs.

---

[8] One of the few cryogenic preservation companies in operation is the Alcor Foundation.

17. Cellular/DNA Repair

Nanotechnology is the science and engineering of mechanical and electronic systems built at atomic dimensions.[9]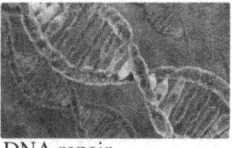
DNA repair

One forecast ability of nanotechnology is its potential for production of self-replicating nano-machines living within individual biological cells.

These artificial enzymes will effect cellular repair, as damage occurs from mechanical causes, radiation, or other aging effects. Repair of DNA ensures genetic stability.

18. Cloning

Biologically-based replication of genetically identical personal copies of yourself, at any time desired, is approaching the possible. Sex is fun, but sexual reproduction is biologically inefficient, suited mainly for inducing genetic variation in species which still advance through the accidents of luck in random combination.

---

[9] The most visible and eloquent proponent of nanotechnology is K. Eric Drexler of MIT and Stanford Universities. His book *Engines of Creation* provides a detailed overview of the held. Other more technical works include:
Drexler, K. Eric. "Molecular Engineering: An Approach to the Development of General Capabilities for Molecular Manipulation." Proc. Natl. Acad. Sci USA, Vol. 78, No. 9, September 1981, pp. 5275-5278.
Drexler, K. Eric. "Rod Logic & Thermal Noise in the Mechanical Nanocomputer." Proc. Third Intl. Symposium on Molecular Electronic Devices, Elsevier North Holland, 1987.
Drexler, K. Eric. "Molecular Engineering: Assemblers and Future Space Hardware:' Aerospace XXI, thirty-third annual meeting of the American Astronomical Society, Paper AAS-86-415.
Feynman, Richard. "There's Plenty of Room at the Bottom." Speech transcript in *Miniaturization*. Gilbert, H. D. (ed.), Reinhold, New York, 1961, pp. 282-296. One of the original works approaching molecular-scale engineering. Nobel Prize-winner Feynman is without a doubt one of the most brilliant scientists of his century.

V. Cybernetic (Post-Biological) Methods for Attaining Immortality [Artificial Life in Silicon]

As the neuromantic cyberpunk author Bruce Sterling notes, evolution moves in clades, radiating outward in omnidirectional diversity, and not following a single linear path. Some silicon visionaries believe that natural evolution of the human species (or at least their branch of it) is near completion. They are no longer interested in merely procreating, but in designing their successors. Carnegie Mellon robot scientist Hans Moravec said, "We owe our existence to organic evolution. But we owe it little loyalty. We are on the threshold of a change in the universe comparable to the transition from non-life, to life."[10]

Human society has now reached a turning point in the operation of the process of evolution, a point at which the next evolutionary step of the species is under our control. Or, more correctly, the next steps, which will occur in parallel, will result in an explosion of diversity of the human species. We are no longer dependent on fitness in any physical sense for survival, our quantum appliances and older mechanical devices provide the requisite means in all circumstances. In the near future, the (now merging) methods of computer and biological technology will make the human form a matter totally determined by individual choice.

As a flesh and blood species we are moribund, stuck at "a local optimum;' to borrow a term from mathematical optimization theory.

Beyond this horizon, which humankind has reached, lies the unknown, the as-yet scarcely imagined. We will design

---

[10] Moravec, Hans. Mind Children: The Future of Robot and Human Intelligence. Harvard University Press, 1988.

our children, and co-evolve intentionally with the cultural artifacts which are our progeny.

Humans already come in some variety of races and sizes. In comparison to what "human" will mean within the next century, we humans are at present as indistinguishable from one another as are hydrogen molecules. Our anthropocentrism will decrease.

We see two principle categorizations of the form of the human of the future, one more biological-like: a bio/machine hybrid of any desired form, and one not biological at all: an "electronic life" on the computer networks. Human-as machine, and human-in-machine.

Of these, human-as-machine is perhaps more easily conceived. Today, we already have crude prosthetic implants, artificial limbs, valves, and entire organs. The continuing improvements in old-style mechanical technology slowly increase the thoroughness of human-machine integration.

The electronic life form of human-in-machine is even more alien to our current conceptions of humanity. Through storage of one's belief systems as on-line data structures, driven by selected control structures (the electronic analog to will?), one's neuronal apparatus will operate in silicon as it did on the wetware of the brain, although faster, more accurately, more self-mutably, and, if desired, immortally.

19. *Archival-Informational*

One standard way of becoming "immortal" is by leaving a trail of archives, biographies, and publicized noble deed.

The increasing presence of stable knowledge media in our Cybernetic Society make this a more rigorous platform for persistent existence. The knowledge possessed by an individual is captured in expert systems, and world-scale hyper-text systems[11] thus ensuring the longevity and accessibility of textural and graphical memes.

Viewed from outside the self, death is not a binary phenomenon, but a continuously varying function. How alive are you in Paris at this moment? In the city in which you live? In the room in which you are reading this?

20. *Head Coach Personality Database Transmission*

Head Coach was a computer system once under development by Futique, Inc.[12], one of the first examples of psychoactive computer software. The program would have allowed the user (performer) to digitize and store thoughts on a routine daily basis. If one leaves, let us say, twenty years of daily computer-stored records of thought-performance, one's grandchildren a century down the line could have "known" and replayed your information habits and mental performances. They would have been able to "share and relive experiences" in considerable detail. To take a most vulgar example, if an individual's moves in a chess game are stored, the descendants can relive, move-by-move, a game played by their great-great-grandmother in the past century.

---

[11] A world-scale hypertext system to permit instantaneous on-line access to global knowledge networks has been envisioned and written about by Ted Nelson in *Literary Machine*, published by the author. Other information is available in Nelson's *Computer Lib*, published in 1974 and republished in 1987 by Microsoft Press.

[12] Timothy Leary coined the term "futique;' which he said is the opposite of antique, when he began designing computer software in the 1980s. Futique was a consortium of artists, writers, programmers, designers, educators, and philosophers all working toward a common goal. When Leary was near the end of (t)his life, he put all his assets IN TRUST for the future-and so Futique, Inc. is now known as The Futique Trust. The trust is principally his archival material which consists of a huge collection of papers and memorabilia from his birth certificate, through all phases of his life and his attention-getting death in 1996. (www.timothylearyarchives.org/futique-trust)

As passive reading is replaced by "active rewriting;" later generations would have been able to relive how we performed the great books of our time.

Yet more intriguing is the possibility of implementing the knowledge extracted over time from a person: their beliefs, preferences, and tendencies, as a set of algorithms guiding a program capable of acting in a manner functionally identical to the person. Advances in robotics technology will take these "turing creatures" away from being mere "brains in bottles" to hybrids capable of interacting sensorilly with the physical world.

21. Nanotech Information Storage: Towards Direct Brain-Computer Transfer

When a computer becomes obsolete, one does not discard the data it contains. The hardware is merely a temporary vehicle of implementation for structures of information. The data gets transferred to new systems for continued use. Decreasing costs of computer storage, CD-ROM and WORM memory systems, mean that no information generated today ever need be lost.

We can consider building an artificial computational substrate both functionally and structurally identical to the brain (and perhaps the body). How? Via the predicted future capabilities of nanotechnology.[13]

Communicating nano-machines which pervade the organism may analyze the neural and cellular structure and transfer the information obtained to machinery capable of growing, atom by atom, an identical copy.

---

[13] We partially regret such speculations beyond present technical capabilities. The brain is a most complex machine, with some 10^{20} individual cells, according to some estimates. Yet we are redeemed by what we see as the technical inevitability of nanotechnology.

But what of the soul? According to the *American Heritage Dictionary*, "soul [is] the animating and vital principle in man credited with the faculties of thought, action and emotion and conceived as forming an immaterial entity distinguishable from but temporarily coexistent with his body."

At first reading this definition seems to be a classic example of theological nonsense. But studied from the perspective of information theory we may be able to wrestle this religio-babble into scientific operations. Let's change the bizarre word "immaterial" to "invisible to the naked senses" i.e., atomic/molecular/electronic. Now the "soul" refers to information processed and stored in microscopic-cellular, molecular packages. Soul becomes any information that "lives;' i.e., is capable of being retrieved and communicated. Is it not true that all the tests for "death" at every level of measurement (nuclear, neural, bodily, galactic) involve checking for unresponsiveness to signals?

From this viewpoint, the twenty-two immortality options become cybernetic methods of preserving one's unique signal capacity. There are as many souls as there are ways storing and communicating data. Tribal lore defines the racial soul. The DNA is a molecular soul. The brain is a neurological soul. Electron storage creates the silicon soul. Nanotechnology makes possible the atomic soul.

22. *Computer Viral: Persistent Existence in Gibson's Cyberspace Matrix*

The previous option permitted personal survival through isomorphic mapping of neural structure to silicon (or some other arbitrary medium of implementation). It also suggests the possibility of survival as an entity in what amounts to a reification of Jung's collective unconscious: the global information network.

In a fictitious twenty-first century imagined by William Gibson, wily cybernauts will not only store themselves electronically, but do so in the form of a "computer virus;' capable of traversing computer networks and of self-replication as a guard against accidental or malicious erasure by others, or other programs. (Imagine the somewhat droll scenario: "What's on this CD?" "Ah, that's just old Leary. Let's go ahead and reformat it.")

Given the ease of copying computer-stored information, one could exist simultaneously in many forms. Where the "I" is in this situation is a matter for philosophy. Our belief is that consciousness would persist in each form, running independently (and ignorant of each other self-manifestation unless in communication with it), cloned at each branch point.

[NOTE: This list of options for Voluntary-Reversible-Metabolic Coma and auto-metamorphosis is not mutually exclusive. The intelligent person needs little encouragement to explore all of these possibilities. And to design many new other alternatives to going belly-up in line with Management Memos.]

Kon-Tiki of the Flesh

In the near future, what is now taken for granted as the perishable human creature will be a mere historical curiosity, one point amidst unimaginable multidimensional diversity of form. Individuals, or groups of adventurers, will be free to choose to reassume flesh-and-blood form, constructed for the occasion by the appropriate science.

Such historical expeditions may well be conducted in the spirit of Thor Heyerdahl's Kon-Tiki voyages. To voyage in what the light of history reveals to be an objectively improbable way, merely to prove that such was possible, as unlikely as it seems.

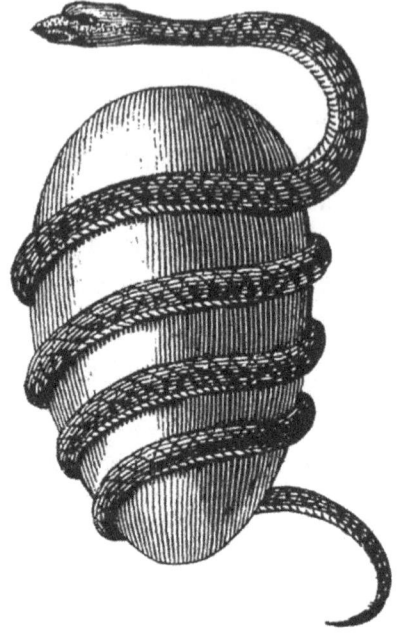

THEURGIA LIBERATIO:
MAGIC AS DIVINE LIBERATION
Chic & S. Tabatha Cicero

"The technique of Magic is one by which the soul flies, straight as an arrow impelled from a taut bow, to serenity, to a profound and impenetrable repose. But it is only man himself who may tauten the string of the bow; none else may accomplish this task for him."

-Israel Regardie
from *The Tree of Life: An Illustrated Study in Magic*

To modern society at large, the subject of magic is one of those hot-button topics that tends to trigger widely differing emotional reactions. Most people undoubtedly believe individuals who practice magic are primitive, superstitious, crazy, or all three. Another segment of the population, specifically religious fundamentalists, believe ALL magic is an evil practice performed by people who, if not evil themselves, are nonetheless the dupes of evil-those who are tricked into performing their unholy rites by the deceptive encouragement of "THE DEVIL:' (Cue ominous music!)

Magic is often described in terms are both scientific and religious, to the consternation of both scientists and clergy. It has been defined as "the method of science, the aim of religion." It is precisely because magic encroaches on the territories of both that it often receives the slings and arrows of the egocentric scientist and the resentful cleric. Of these two groups, however, the criticism originating from the indignant clergy is the more shrill, hateful, and uniformed. Yet magic is only one of the more recent recipients of these attacks. Not long ago the science of mathematics was considered a form of sorcery, and mathematicians were viewed with suspicion.

What is it about the practice of magic that makes fundamentalists condemn it so?

Beyond the obvious fact that humans often denounce what they do not understand, there is also the undisputed fact that magical practice flies directly in the face of the fundamentalist's agenda: to proselytize, to convert, and to persuade as many people as possible to think the same way, pray the same prayers, worship the same deity, attend the same churches, listen to the same pastors, and fill the same coffers. For centuries, Western theocrats have based their agenda on Constantine's fourth century approach: One Emperor, One Empire, One God, One Religion. One unified bureaucracy ruling it all. One particular set of Christian beliefs was exalted and all others condemned. Deviation was discouraged, to put it mildly. Other forms of worship were exiled, died out, or went underground. This was the religious reality of the West for centuries until cracks started to appear in the theological door, nailed into place by Luther's hammer.

New Christian sects soon flourished, but most also embraced Constantine's approach-there was one right set of beliefs and all others were wrong. Each sect taught that it alone had the One True Way, and all other sects were deceived, blinkered, misinformed, or bound for hell. Adherents were taught that following the instructions of the church (whichever sect it happened to be) would result in happiness and salvation. Following a different church could result in damnation and eternal misery. Such was the kindling that sparked religious conflicts such as the Thirty Years War and the Inquisition.

With the Renaissance came a resurgence in classical knowledge and philosophy. The Age of Reason (seventeenth century) and the Age of Enlightenment (eighteenth century) followed and built on the scientific advancements of preceding ages. In ways never been previously possible, more and more people began to examine their deepest-held beliefs concerning God, religion, and humanity's relationship to the Divine. Influential thinkers of the day began an intellectual revolution against the yoke of religious orthodoxy-sometimes quietly, sometimes vociferously. As evidenced by such documents as Pope Leo XIII's "Human Genus: Against Freemasonry and Spirit of the Age" (1884), which condemned such ideas as "democracy"–power over individual human lives gradually slipped away from church, which kicked and screamed at every lost bit of control and authority.

It was against this backdrop that the nineteenth century "Occult Revival" was born, ushering in a proliferation of esoteric societies and such thinkers as Eliphas Levi, Helena Blavatsky, W. Wynn Westcott, S. L. MacGregor Mathers, Aleister Crowley, Arthur Edward Waite, and others. At the heart of this revival was the study of magic; a yearning for liberation of the human spirit through arcane knowledge.

THE LIBERATING PROPERTIES OF MAGIC

The magic of the West is often described as hermetic, named for an ancient magician known as Hermes Trismegistus, the legendary author of several books on the occult sciences, whose name is in turn derived from the messenger god Hermes. One of the principle aims of magic is the

1. Arthur Edward Waite 2. S.L. MacGregor Mathers
3. W. Wynn Westcott   4. Helena Blavatsky

elevation/ evolution of the human psyche to its highest potential. For some this may allude to an inner communication with a subjective part of the self, often called the Higher Self, the Soul, or the Higher and Divine Genius. Others take this to mean a more objective state of communication and guidance under the name of Holy Guardian Angel, Daemon, or "inner planes contact." The methods used to facilitate this communication include the study and performance of various occult sciences grouped together under the banner of magic.

Magic is the art and science of causing change to occur in conformity with will. This change can occur: 1) in the outer, manifest world, 2) in the magician's consciousness, and 3) most often in both, for changing one often changes the other. Magical change occurs in a way that is not currently understood by modern science because it works through the Unmanifest through subtle manipulations of the invisible, spiritual realms. However, the workings of magic are subject to natural law. The effects of magic are sometimes clearly visible in the physical world, but other times they are only apparent on a personal, spiritual level. The workings of magic are not limited by the constraints of time and space.

Magic is liberated from the current conventions of material science, although science may someday understand how and why magic works. Magic is also liberated from the concepts of time and space, because the astral realms where magic works are constrained by neither.

In ancient times magic and religion were regarded as one and the same: they shared a fundamental origin and unity. However, modern magic, which can be considered a refinement of "medieval magic" is entirely distinct from religion- it is *technique* as opposed to belief. The separation of magic from religion in the West occurred primarily because of the prohibition against magic by a domineering church. But it also resulted partly from a truce that Renaissance humanists were forced to make with religious leaders–namely, that the church was the sole authority on the Divine and the heavenly powers, while the natural (mundane) world, including the celestial spheres and the elements, fell under the purview of the scientist and the philosopher. Esoteric thinkers such as Marsilio Ficino had to maintain that magical workings involved purely natural forces that did not infringe upon the domain claimed by the church. This unsteady cease fire was successful for a brief time until rebellious humanists such as Pico della Mirandola pushed the envelope with the study of Qabalah and its myriad of angels, archangels and divine emanations-all of which magicians use effect change.

Methods of magic include invocation, evocation, divination, the creation and consecration of talismans, skrying and other forms of astral work, vibration, meditation, visualization, and ceremonial ritual. Magic has its own set of attributes, mental processes, and natural laws, whereas religion depends more on faith, creed, and official doctrine. In short, religion is a *specific belief* or set of beliefs, values, and practices usually based on the teachings of a spiritual leader. Magic is a *method or mechanism* of causing change to occur in the material world in accordance with cosmic laws. In a very simplified analogy, magic inclines toward *thinking and doing* while religion gravitates toward *feeling and being*. The two are very definitely related, but they are not identical. The yearning for the supernatural propels them both, though in different ways.

Organized religion tends to limit access to the supernatural world within the bulwark of a formalized theology, and the faithful are strongly encouraged to remain within that framework. In magic, however, the individual is encouraged to experience the supernatural realms for him or herself. While religion often focuses on the group experience, group-think and group interdependence, usually with a single religious leader or small group of leaders shepherding their flock, magic emphasizes the individual experience, independent thought, and belief that is based on personal revelation of the Divine. These are qualities that the magic shares with mysticism.

In her book *Practical Occultism* Evelyn Underhill described mysticism as "... the art of union with Reality. The mystic is a person who has attained that union in greater or less degree; or who aims at and believes in such attainment." This goal is no less than the Completion of the Great Work espoused by magicians. The primary methods used by mystics are prayer, devotion, meditation, and contemplation. However, mystics such as Underhill have been known to be every bit as unsympathetic toward magic as are orthodox clergy. Concerning these esoteric sibling rivalries, Dion Fortune set the record straight in her book *Esoteric Orders and Their Work* by comparing the mystic and the magician,

> It is amusing to note that, while the occultist decries the spiritualist, the mystic looks askance at the occultist; yet a mystic is simply an introvert occultist, and the occultist an extrovert mystic. Both aim at the same goal, though they seek it by different methods. The difference between them is of temperament, not of ideal. When the scientific temperament approaches the Unseen, it chooses to Occult Path of development, and when the artistic temperament approaches the Unseen, it chooses the Mystic Path; one progresses through right knowing and the other through right feeling, and both meet in the end. Difference of method should never blind us to unity of aim.
>
> The mystic pursues a solitary path, even when he is a member of a community; his visions are for himself alone, and he has often but little power to teach that which he has himself learnt. He reaches the heights of the spirit and dwells there apart; his experience is a personal one, and cannot be communicated to others. He is essentially the artistic temperament working upon the things of the spirit; creative, joyous, and inspiring to those who can appreciate his art because they are akin to him in nature. Esotericism, without a touch of mystic rapture, would be as drab as a culture that had no place for the beautiful; but a spiritual culture which is purely mystical has little

relation to the problems of humanity and no message for the common man.

Occultism, on the other hand, is of the intellect. The occult path is followed in cooperation with others, because its heights are achieved by means of group-work and the use of ritual.

While mysticism represents a passive path, magic is the active path of spiritual liberation. It is often called theurgy or "God-working" because the magician is an active participant in his or her own quest to approach the Light of the Divine and the profound peace of illumination. What is certain is while many true, sincere mystics are not magicians, many true, sincere magicians are also mystics.

THE PSYCHOLOGICAL LIBERATION OF MAGIC

In addition to its spiritual qualities, there is another useful property of magic-theurgy as a tool for psychological liberation. Israel Regardie, in *The Middle Pillar: The Balance Between Mind and Body*, compared the sublimating effects of magical work to the healing of the mind/psyche garnered by psychotherapy,

> Analytical psychology and magic comprise in my estimation two halves or aspects of a single technical system. Just as the body and mind are not two separate units, but are simply the dual manifestations of an interior dynamic 'something; so psychology and magic comprise similarly a single system whose goal in the integration of the human personality. Its aim is to unify the different departments and functions of man's being, to bring into operation those which previously for various reasons were latent. Incidentally, its technique is such that neurotic symptoms which were too insistent upon expression either become illuminated or toned down by a process of equilibration.

The goal of both magic and psychotherapy is the growth and well being of the individual on every level-physical, mental, and psychological. But one element is missing from modern psychology–the spiritual essence of humanity and divine character of life. Theurgy includes what psychology had long forgotten–the spiritual welfare of the individual.

Inner alchemy is another field closely related to our discussion. The alchemist works to separate, purify, and recombine the principle components of whatever substance being worked with-whether the object of his work is a base metal, an organic substance, or their own human soul. The fundamental objective is integration, or the liberation of the base material from the limitations (and illusions) of separateness, a goal alchemy shares with both psychotherapy and magic. All three fields can be said to involve three similar stages of progression. In alchemy these stages are called separation, purification, and cohobation (recombination). In psychology they are referred to as analysis, confrontation (of the shadow), and individuation (self-realization). In magic these stages are often called purification, consecration, and union (with the Higher Self). All are simply different terms for the same essential experience: liberation of one's highest human potential. However, the sacerdotal art of magic is the most direct and inspired.

As is often the case, no author is more eloquent on the subject than Israel Regardie, who says in his book Foundations of *Practical Magic: An Introduction to Qabalistic, Magical and Meditative Techniques*,

> [Magic] deals with that sphere of the psyche of which normally we are not conscious but which exerts an enormous influence upon our lives. Magic is a series of psychological techniques so devised as to enable us to probe

Dr. Israel Regardie

more deeply into ourselves. To what end? First, that we shall understand ourselves more completely. Apart from the fact that such self-knowledge in itself is desirable, an understanding of the inner nature releases us from unconscious compulsions and motivations and confers a mastery over life. Second, that we may the more fully express that inner self in everyday activities. It is only when men and women have reached, or perhaps when the more advanced men and women in the world have evolved, some degree of inner realization that we may ever hope for that ideal utopian condition of things–a wide tolerance, peace, and universal brotherhood. It is to such as these that Magic owes its *raison d'etre*.

INITIATION: A NEW BEGINNING

For those who seek to actively work with those of a like mind, initiation is the preliminary step into the realm of magic. From ancient times up to the present today, initiation ceremonies have played a major role in mystery traditions and magical groups. Spiritual seekers of the past were drawn to the rites of Isis and Osiris, Eleusis, Samothrace, and Orpheus because of the sense of spiritual vigor and euphoria they provided through elaborate initiation ceremonies.

The word initiation means "to begin." Magical initiation into a specific magical group represents the passage into a distinctly esoteric mind-set and spiritual outlook. The Western Magical Tradition encompasses many branches of the Hermetic Tree–Khemetic, Hellenic, Gnostic, Neo-Platonic, Qabalistic, Alchemical, Rosicrucian, Golden Dawn, Thelemic, Ogdoadic, etc. Teaching organizations and mystery schools can be found for all of these respective paths.

The advantages of group work are many. Mystery schools past and present were founded by individuals motivated by any number of reasons, but the best are usually inspired to teacher, whether by inner planes contacts or divine muse, to offer a useful curriculum of esoteric work that can guide the student step-by-step through the magical/alchemical process of purification, consecration, and union. To be an Initiate means one is accepted into an inner circle whose teachings and rituals are meaningful only to other members of the group who share this common experience. According to Dion Fortune, "Students of esoteric science have always tended to band themselves together into caravans for the purpose of taking the Golden Journey." Admittance to such a group confers a sense of fellowship and belonging, of receiving arcane information, and of having been uplifted through the disclosure of divinely inspired wisdom. "The occultist goes by a well-marked way which has been trodden by countless feet from time immoral:' This does not mean the would-be spiritual rebel simply trades in one congregation for another. A magical order is not a religion and is not designed to take the place of religion, although religious symbolism is often used in ceremonies as a catalyst to stimulate the alchemical process of self-evolution. The rite of initiation is meant to purify the candidate and prepare him or her to receive the teachings of the group, which can aid and support one's personal process of illumination. Ultimately, however, the Initiate is in control of his or her own destiny. Spiritual attainment within a magical group still depends on the individual will, perseverance, merits, and character of the student.

MAGICAL INITIATION: FOUR PITFALLS TO AVOID

Magicians often describe the wonderful experiences they have had during initiation or as a result of initiation into the mysteries. For most, initiations are deeply inspiring, meaningful, and even cathartic experiences. However, as in all things, there can be a downside to magical initiation. In his article "The Darker Side of Initiation," Donald Michael Kraig listed four dangers the student should be aware of when seeking out initiation into any magical group: failure, fakes, abuse, and self-deception. These four pitfalls threaten the spiritual liberation the student is searching for. Here we will examine each of these hazards in turn.

1. Failure: Liberation Short-Circuited

A large proportion of people who join magical groups will never make it all the way through the grade system of whatever group they have joined. This is a true, simple fact. Most leaders of magical groups will tell you the percentage of people who persevere and continue on to work the highest grades of their respective system is less than ten percent; sometimes much less.

We are certainly not saying that who leaves a particular magical group is "blowing" their chance at spiritual liberation. True magical liberation is personal and can only come from within–it is not dependant on any group. There are many good reasons students leave magical groups: health reasons, distance issues, family obligations, work-related time constraints, changes in one's religious outlook, spiritual path changes, etc. A student may leave a specific magical group and find another that is more suitable to his or her spiritual needs. We are not talking about that here.

Liberation short-circuited is failure to launch. Some people leave a magical group because of their own faulty expectations of what magic, initiation, or group work entails. Students drop out only to denounce that the group had any value whatsoever, sometimes writing off magic entirely. Some go so far as to condemn what they were previously involved in. In cases such as this, the ex-student does not recognize that the true failure was either in his or her own lack of authentic, inner initiation or their own misunderstanding of the experience. They also falsely assume because the magic did not work for them, it will not work for anybody else.

One example of this was a student who left our Order shortly after receiving a Neophyte initiation, because she had expected to see and experience the hand of God literally reaching down and embracing her during the initiation. She was very disappointed when the hand did not appear! Failure to Launch.

Another example was a student who wanted to invoke Enochian entities while he was still in the Outer Order, against our advice. (While some Outer Order students may be magically advanced enough to do this, we were certain this particular student was not.) This was a classic case of "lust for results" or performing complex magical workings just to "see what happens." In nearly every case of this kind, students involved don't really believe that magic is real, and so they perform advanced theurgical workings they are not ready for, precisely because they want to experience the kind of magical "special effects" seen in Hollywood movies about the occult. In our example, the student in question was frightened when he opened psychological doors he was totally unprepared to deal with. He dropped out of the Order and swore off magic entirely.

The end result of magical failure to launch is a feeling of general negativity, pessimism, and possibly depression that can last for quite a long time.

2. Fakes: Liberation Mislead

Fraternal organizations and magical groups have a long tradition of tracing their hereditary roots back to the esoteric societies and archaic religions of earlier times–to the sixteenth century Rosicrucians, the medieval Knights Templar, the ancient Israelites, the Egyptians, the Babylonians, and even the inhabitants of Atlantis, lost in the mists of time. While these various legends of ancient initiatory lineages can provide inspiration, allegorical drama, and symbolic knowledge that can be of great value to the Initiate, they almost always breakdown under the scrutiny of historical fact.

For several decades (if not centuries) wild claims made by esoteric leaders, fraternities, and magical groups of all stripes have misled countless spiritual seekers. Fake lineages, claims of unique apostolic succession, and outrageous assertions of superhuman powers have become so common among magical groups vying for members that the image of the charlatan magician or con artist guru is almost a proverb.

The founders of the Golden Dawn were not guilt free in this respect, since most reputable Golden Dawn scholars have concluded that Westcott's continental contact "Fraulein

Sprengel" was invented to give the fledging Order a proper pedigree for its era. We can absolve Westcott's sin because we believe the end result–the creation of the Golden Dawn was positive and useful.

What is far less forgivable is the repetition of such creation myths by modern day myth makers who fabricate a magical apostolic succession stretching back nearly to the prehistoric age. These are the magicians and groups who wear their empty claims of superiority on their sleeve and boast of having an impressive lineage or charter they never show to anyone, lest they be discovered to be the frauds that they are. As far as spiritual teachers go, these are generally the ones who publicly claim Christ-like piety while privately behaving like frat boys gone wild.

If this sounds like an unfair critique of those who pad their magical resumes in order to dupe their followers, it is certainly not the first of its kind. We can turn to many of the great esoteric thinkers of the past to hear harsher assessments. In *Esoteric Orders and Their Work*, Dion Fortune warned "Such groups are innumerable at the present time, and may either represent the door ajar, or a snare and a delusion..." William Gray, author of *Inner Traditions of Magic*, advised seekers to,

> ...be highly suspicious of all demands for money or pretentious claims made on material levels... It is best to avoid commercialism in any form of disguise if genuine spiritual development is sought. No matter what chicanery is used to camouflage money-motive and power policies, they remain today what they always were, traps that lead Light seekers into confusion and disorders of the worst kind...

In *Words of Wisdom*, Manly P. Hall offers one of the most cutting indictments of all, calling them "metaphysical carpetbaggers who are indeed parasites which have attached themselves to the tree of philosophy." Hall tells us that "the fraudulent metaphysician is usually finally convicted by his own words and actions," and that his misrepresentations usually fall into a few easily detected categories,

> He is generally the only possessor of some very superlative truth which he has received direct from... some equally august source difficult to check on... He is willing to communicate this extraordinary knowledge to anyone who has... dollars, in ten easy lessons which inevitably lead to adeptship... He nearly always implies that possession of the peculiar knowledge of which he is the sole owner (copyright applied for) will inevitably cause the individual fortunate enough to receive his instruction to become healthy, wealthy, and wise...

Would such "peculiar knowledge" and questionable lineage be valuable to one's magical liberation if it karmically linked the student to a teacher whose words and actions run completely opposite to the ideals, principles, and ethics he or she claims to uphold? Unfortunately, the second pitfall of magical initiation *(liberation mislead)*, often goes hand-in-hand with the next hazard-abuse.

3. Abuse: Liberation vs. Enslavement

The practice of magic is an important avenue for personal liberation and spiritual evolution. How ironic is it then, that when prospective students attempt to seek out legitimate schools of magic they sometimes run the risk of entangling themselves with a group that is not so much "occult" as it is "a cult?" What about teachers or groups that claim to instruct students in the liberating techniques of magic, and then proceed to drain students' bank accounts, interfere with their personal lives, demand absolute obedience, or take over their free will?

In such scenarios the rational for magic gets turned on its head-liberation is transformed into enslavement; the enslavement of naive seekers by unscrupulous gurus and abusive "spiritual leaders." How does the aspiring magical "rebel" avoid being duped into becoming just another compliant sheep in a submissive herd, waiting to get fleeced?

This is no new problem. More than a century ago, Dion Fortune warned readers to stay clear of dodgy groups and teachers. She advised students to look for three things in a reputable teacher: right principles, genuine knowledge, and "such common sense and capacity as shall prevent a teacher from involving his pupils in muddles and misadventures." Fortune goes on to say,

> ... for all practical purposes the neophyte is pretty much in the hands of his initiator at the outset, and if the senior occultist's power is abused, the neophyte is in for an unpleasant experience, to say the least of it. The true initiator will no more exercise undue influence over his pupil nor abuse his superior knowledge than will the honourable doctor over his patient nor the honourable lawyer over his client; but there are black sheep in every profession, and the occult world; unfortunately, is not sufficiently organized to permit of its black sheep being officially deprived of their power to practise. Therefore the would-be pupil has to look to himself pretty sharply, especially in his early days before he knows the ropes.

Abuse in occult circles usually starts with unreasonable demands for unquestioning obedience to a single leader. Again, the original Golden Dawn was not blameless in this regard: S. L. MacGregor Mathers made such a demand of the London Adepts, going so far as to expel one member, Annie Horniman, even after she submitted to his demands. (This event, as much as any other, helped to sow the seeds of discord, which finally led to the Order's break-up in 1903. It was also a bone-headed move since Horniman was Mathers' financial benefactor. Shortly after he expelled her, Mathers and his wife asked Horniman for more money!)

It is essential students be able to discern the difference between a legitimate group that will foster the Candidate's spiritual growth and one that exists primarily to benefit the leader(s) of the group. Students should steer well clear of groups that exploit students in terms of money, power, sexual gratification, etc.

Abusive behavior in esoteric groups can be relatively harmless, as was the case with S. L. MacGregor Mathers' demands (the main result of which was the implosion of the Order), or it can be harmful in the extreme. The poster child for everything that can go horribly wrong in such a group was the Order of the Solar Temple, a doomsday cult responsible for the deaths of seventy-four of its followers in Quebec, Switzerland, and France between 1994 and 1997.

The only way for the student to know for certain whether a group is sincere or abusive is to ask specific questions of people in the wider esoteric community. Questions such as: Does the group exhibit excessive devotion or fanatical dedication to some person, idea, or goal? Does it use manipulative techniques of persuasion and control? Do the group's leaders encourage isolation from family and friends? Do group leaders actively promote the break-up of relationships? Does the organization exert powerful group pressures, information management, and other methods to suspend the individual's critical judgment? Do the leaders of the organization promote complete dependency on the group and the fear or consequences of leaving it? Do the leaders demand subservience or an unreasonable amount of work to be done for "the good of the group?" Does the goal of the group seem designed to benefit the group's leaders to the actual or possible detriment of members? Do the leaders of the group continually ask members for money or donations? Do the leaders of the group regularly engage in acts of harmful magic and/or smear campaigns against others, or encourage their members to engage in such acts? Does the leader make unreasonable demands for absolute obedience from his or her students? Vigilant students can save themselves years of stress, disappointment, and heartache by finding out the answers to these important questions. According to Dion Fortune there is also the option of self-initiation, which is always open to the student of the Mysteries,

> The solitary worker, depending on aspiration and meditation; and unguided save by his intuition, although his progress may be slower, is in a much better position than the blind follower of a blind leader.
> Remember that it is always better to be alone than in bad company, and that you need never fear that your occult progress will be retarded by a sacrifice made on the altar of principle.

4. Self-Deception: Liberation Unrecognized

The final hazard to be avoided is self-deception, which can be the most subtle and difficult challenge of all. Self-deception can take many forms; from the student who takes an initiation and thinks that he or she instantly gains great psychic or magical powers, to the teacher whose ego expands to messianic proportions. People who are natural clairvoyants and mediums are especially susceptible, as are those with chemical imbalances or other psychological problems. As ironic as it sounds, a healthy dose of skepticism is required to safely traverse the astral planes where magic is worked. Magicians must be scientists of the mind-testing every visionary experience for kernels of truth and husks of delusion. Without taking the proper precautions it becomes far too easy for some to lose their way in the ethereal realms. They run the risk of becoming "astral junkies" unable to distinguish divine revelation from flights of fantasy-spiritual breakthrough from psychic breakdown.

The practice of magic works to release latent energy from the subconscious and expand the mind's horizons. As the magician becomes proficient in the theurgical arts he or she undergoes an increase in psychic awareness, knowledge, and self-confidence. This is often accompanied by feelings of new life-purpose and direction. But magic can also sometimes reawaken the mechanism of the infantile mega-ego, causing delusions of grandeur and self-importance. In this case, the rebel simply becomes a slave to a new Master: the all-consuming Ego.

Balance and common sense must be maintained in order to keep self-deception and egomania at bay. This is absolutely crucial to the magician's spiritual wellbeing.

LIBERATION FULFILLED

"When I speak here of Magic I have reference to the Divine Theurgy praised and reverenced by antiquity. It is of a quest spiritual and divine that I write; a task of self-creation and recreation, the bringing into human life of something eternal and enduring."
- Israel Regardie
from *The Tree of Life: An Illustrated Study in Magic*

So long as the magician avoids the perils mentioned earlier, the "Golden Journey" should be an infinitely rewarding one. Genuine magical initiation-where effects in the interior world have a significant impact on a person's life-is authentic and liberating. These are the initiations that change lives, sometimes in the most unexpected ways. The Path of Initiation, carefully and intelligently trodden, can be one of the most important steps taken by the spiritual rebel. In magic, the Initiate is expected to man the helm of his own ship. While others may check the compass and provide guidance, ultimately it is up to the individual magician to check the star-charts and set his or her course into the mystic.

TEAM PSYCHOPATH
Peter Conte

Gimme a "P"... gimme an "S"... gimme a ... wait... why am I going on like this? Revving you up, Kid. Gotta score. Gotta win. The big game–Your Life–hangs in the balance. You're the Team and this is Training Camp. If you're not looking, feeling, being sharp, you lose. And you're not a loser, are you?

The Opposition hates you. Holding you back, calling you strange, saying you're stupid, always kicking your meager ass, they can't stand that you're defiant, of them, and everything. The game has to be played their way and that's it. There's no room in their world for someone like you.

Tough, hey? You are different. They whack you one, you whack them back. They don't even know the meaning of pain. You're Hell on earth, and everyone and everything is the enemy.

Take it as it comes, give it back triple. Fight to the end.

Well, hopefully, the end is a long way off. You have a lot of terrorizing, er ... living, to do. And *The Black Books*[1] will help. This is the Game Plan and the Masters didn't write it just to watch you putz along. They expect you to execute, to attain, to evoke your Will, and wreak joyful havoc on the world around you. You can take all of the hints, rules, and slights on your character written in the *Black Books* and

---

[1] *The Black Books* (New Falcon Publications) comprise a multi-volume series of booklets written by Dr. Christopher S. Hyatt, Ph.D. that coincide with the teachings of the Extreme Individual Institute, which Hyatt founded. Following Dr. Hyatt's death in 2008 the EII was renamed as the New Extreme Individual Institute, and is a non-profit/prophet (ir)religious sleeper cell, dedicated to the furtherance of the work of the EII. (www.neweii.com)

actualize into a working marvel, a formidable Magician, a Psychopath. But you gotta be in shape.

What's your Team look like? Hell, Kid, like you. Mind, body, senses, emotions, that's your Team. And whether you like it or not, the Team has to be beaten into fighting shape. You gotta be cruel to be cruel. It's the Psychopath's way. The harder you are on yourself, the less the world can control you. The more personal pain applied to yourself, the stronger your Magick over the Food/Prey. Set your own pain threshold, the higher the better. Because you can take it, you will succeed. Time to fight, time to win, gotta get to it before time runs out. Go Team!

Coach sez: enough already Conte. Don't you ever get tired of sniffing your own Brain Farts?

Only a Star can lead the Team and that's your BMOC (Big Mind On Campus). You have the biggest Mind around. Just ask you. You'll tell them. The Psychopathic Mind is quick, incisive, and deadly, a seething volcano held on standby, capable of seeing everything and able to switch on automatically to act and counteract adjusting to the unfolding human drama progressing in real time while preparing a course of action to implement as to whatever will be happening in the next few seconds. And at the very best you won't even notice the Mind working. Properly trained, your Mind will calmly click on and guide the body around all obstacles, and then go back into Ready Mode. The Psychopath's Mind needs to be ever vigilant, to react quickly, and to handle many threats at the same time. Daydreaming is deadly. Do your daydreaming in your Alone Time where all scenarios of what can happen, what might go wrong, and what you really want can be computed. Dream big and imagine glory. Also, erase the past Imprinting that's ravaging your Mind. Mental baggage is a lead weight and slows your Team. Keep a blank

Mind in your present day circumstances to prevent further negative Imprinting. The only allowed Imprinting is your Mind programming for success.

Live in your daily life as usual with the stipulation of now you will be moving in a Psychopathic way. Take the training hints in the *Black Book* and win.

Observe only, don't think. Observing with a blank Mind allows for taking in and reacting to all the actions around you. Only actively think when confronted with a concrete problem, and then go back on standby again. It's more important to guide the senses then to dwell on the meaning of life. Your life is War.

The Brain is your CIC (Combat Information Center) that the Mind can trust to operate independently by virtue of the previous programming agreed to between them during operational exercises to set up the flow charts necessary to allow the Team to work as a whole. The less damage you do to your Brain, the better off you'll be. Alcohol, drugs, and bad Magick gone wrong dents the Brain, but, Hell, a Psychopath has to have a little fun, right?

The Brain seethes with electrical power. Try this exercise: when walking at night try to put the streetlights out. Later on, try to do this to a whole room. It will work and scare the hell out of people. You might get a minor headache, well; sometimes it's excruciating, but think of the power involved. Use this power in your Magical Workings.

Coach sez: keep your Game in the Mind.

The burning essence of everyone's Soul rests just inside the pupils of the Eyes. Power emanates outwards attacking all that comes in contact with their gaze and sucking in the wavering Wills of those caught in their trap. Normal eyesight talks of the person's Mind, Psychopathic eyesight is silent. Pull your vision awareness back in from the pupils.

This creates "quiet eyes" and no info will escape to tell what you're thinking.

Learn to have a "soft focus" (peripheral vision). This allows you see from ear to ear without anyone knowing that you're looking around. The more info you ingest, the better the Mind operates. Knowledge is power. Take in all you can see and give nothing away. In your Alone Time work on connecting the Eyes to the Brain so that the Mind can program them to perform the proper operations called for. Let your Eyes cast your Spells.

Coach sez: you can't spell Evil without the EYE.

The Nose is a psychic antenna able to sniff out the fears and desires of others. Try this exercise: turn off the other senses and let the Nose tell you what's going on around you.

Remember to breathe. If you're not breathing, you're probably dead and that can ruin all of the fun you expect to experience. Proper breathing exercises can help control the Mind and Body and mute your reactions to what others are doing to you.

Coach sez: know how to NOSE out the other Team's plays.

The Ears alert you as to what's happening around you from nearby to the far horizon. When they activate, they override all the other senses and send a message to the Mind to alert the Body to be ready in case defensive actions are called for. Constantly pounding the Ears with loud noises and music will severely damage them and leave you at a serious disadvantage.

Coach sez: tell those WIDE RECEIVERS to stay alert.

This triple threat combination of the Eyes, Nose, and Ears constitute your Early Warning System. By having a quiet essence about you, they can very effectively flare up individually or together and alert the Mind to all dangers.

Coach sez: D #.

The Mouth deals with Taste, Expressions, and Speech and is designated the Special Teams Package. The Star player is the Tongue. This tasteful little Devil is always in the thick of the action, and is a major pleasure center.

The naked, little Taste Buds chant "yum, yum, yum" as they come, come, come from whatever Mother Tongue has to offer when Father Mouth opens up and the sky is blotted out from all the delights that drop on to their seething world. They can go on forever. Beware the trap of the Space Masters who extol you to consume "Mass Quantities" as you could become Jabba the Hutt.

Coach sez: have a TASTE for the Good Life.

As a Signal Center to the world, the Lips let others know whether to approach or stay away, and the Emotional or Psychological state that you're going through at the moment.

Liken the Lips to the hiking of the ball, when they move the face follows. Only extreme effort can keep the Lips from reacting to what the Eyes see. When the Mind has concrete control of all operations, then are the Lips silent, but you'll be accused of having a dour attitude and a droll sense of humor.

Coach sez: tell'em to wrap their LIPS around this!

It is said Speech separates Humans from the rest of the creatures on this Planet. Not so. Have you never had a cat screech at you for its dinner? But Selective Speech does separate the Psychopath from the rest of the world. Whereas the Food/Prey babbles on, the Psychopath knows the secret of the Five Second Rule. Whatever you think, feel, or want to say, wait five seconds before you actually speak. That way you're not one of the babbling idiots whose words are unnecessary, inane, or end up ignored, and you'll either look like a genius from the validity of your point or your words were going to be babble so you kept quiet.

In fact, the less you say the more power you'll retain. Use your words to guide the conversation and by such the Food/Prey in the direction you want things to go. Use speech as a battering ram, drop subtle comments, invoke humor to entrance, tease, cajole, vary your cadence, and so on. Work out patterns in your Alone Time. Some styles of communication will be easy for you. Stick with them. Overcome fear with a Public Speaking class, or get a sales counter job where you have to deal with the public.

Large gatherings are the Psychopath's hunting ground. Well, they're everyone's hunting ground, but it depends on how you view them. The air is filled with crescendos of loud yapping. Usually, when the Mouth is moving, the Mind is closed down. Control your Speech. The Psychopath must keep the Ears open for guide words like the NSA does. A key word will alert you as to the presence of a Food/Prey. Hear, and then hunt.

Being out in the world might have you banging your head off the wall, but too much Alone Time is worse. All living creatures need to talk. Our words are the footpaths that lead us along from one moment to the next. Let your words be incisive.

Coach sez: We'll Kill'em with the RUN and SHOOT.

There's nothing you can do about the Weather, or your

Moods. Rarely good, almost always depressing, a Mood can settle on you from out of nowhere. When it hits, you're out of commission, hopefully for not that long. Even a Psychopath is human (unfortunately).

Coach sez: Goddamn Rain.

Your fan Base, the Emotions, love you, sometimes. Living vicariously through you, they expect a win, but usually they're not helping things. All your hard work for control can be ripped apart in an instant by their selfish hungers. This screaming crowd seethes about demanding your immediate attention. Rage, love, happiness, despair, lust, gluttony, and an infinite viper's den wearing your colors roots for you, but they're only on your side if you give them precedence over the others.

They scream out their existence to the world, me, me, me! The sudden violent force they exert takes over the Game. One of these monsters is enough; let alone having a multitude manifest at the same time. When they rear their screeching heads, you're no longer the Hunter, but something to be avoided.

A Hermetic exercise to help control these Demons is to imagine you have a Pendulum in your Mind that will swing to and fro when you get emotional. If you don't let yourself get too far UP when you're excited, then you won't get that far DOWN when things go wrong. Control your swing when good things are happening even though this mutes the level of happiness. You can't control the DOWN side of the swing on its own. The Pendulum can be made to have a tight swing. You'll only be as DOWN as you let yourself get UP.

By establishing control over the Emotions, then you can conjure them up whenever you want. It can be mighty exciting, for you, not the Food/Prey, when you go through your roladex and pick out an Emotion to display. It'll scare the Hell out of them, leaving them wondering "where did that come from?" This might be considered "playing with your food." Sudden Emotional outbursts, controlled with the connivance of the Mind, will create confusion in the Food/Preys and this is one of the Psychopath's feeding zones. It's fun to go crazy at the push of a button.

Coach sez: look at those Crazy Bastards. At least they're good for the Beer Sales.

Your "LOOK" is your Uniform, which sets the Style of how you appear to the world. From the wildest eccentricity to the conformity to your selected group, the Psychopath is adamant that "things" must be "just right" Color (black?, again?) of clothing, type of jewelry, hair style, accessories (do something about those shoes, Kid), all scream in the face of the world at large, the world the Psychopath rebels from, but is all this excess really rebellion?

It could be that a white T-shirt and blue jeans might just make you the most dangerous person around. The true Psychopathic Hunter embraces invisibility, and if you look "lame" that's all they'll notice about you, and then no one will fear you, and that's when everyone should be very, very afraid. They won't know where their whackings are coming from.

But that probably won't be the case. The Psychopath, especially an Occult one, has to have at least a little "weirdness." Just remember, the badges and codes shown on your LOOK alert the Roll Models as to who and what you are, and make it easy for "the Man" to bust your balls. If you exert all your energy fighting, you'll not be able to feed in peace.

Wearing Gothic in a Goth crowd is conformity. Wearing Gothic in a Brooks Brother's crowd stands out. Wearing Brooks Brother's in a Goth crowd is Psychopathic. Or you can a get a Tattoo.

Coach sez: do that Crazy End Zone Dance.

Your Quirks are your Playbook, Kid. What'a ya got? Do you stand like a lump, or flash green at the Bartender? If the line isn't moving, is it you holding things up? Work the Red Zone. How you use your Body sets you apart from all the other Psychopaths. Run some good Routes.

Coach sez: dazzle 'em with the ol' Shake and Bake.

The Game will be played on the Field of Action, your Body. There's not a lot you can do about how your Body looks. Deal with what you got. A huge Body can be graceful, and a lithe one klutzy. You don't have to be comfortable about your shape, just confident from that Psychopathic inner vibe. Motion, with attitude, allows you to shine.

Your Body is you-in-the-world. Your Flesh seeks other Flesh to actualize its existence. It's the way of Nature. Often, ignoring better judgment, it seeks some down and dirty action. You'll have to be a great Grounds keeper to get it back in to somewhat pristine shape, but don't worry about wearing it out.

From the moment of your Birth, your cells have raged a War between Life and Death. Whether you lock yourself in a room, or ingest all of the poisons available to you, there is nothing you can do to halt your inevitable demise. Buck up, Kid, all of us are Walking Corpses. So, allow your Body to enjoy total fulfillment, for it'll be staying here even as the Mind travels on to a Better Game.

Coach sez: the Game was decided by SUDDEN DEATH.

Listen up, Kid, this is the Unhappy Recap. No one's rooting for you. What you gain, they lose. You're on your own. Gotta grab with some gusto everything you want. Their only hope is that you'll wake up tomorrow and play the same lame game. Gimme a "P"... gimme an "S"...

Coach sez: hehehe...

Aleister Crowley

Lon Milo DuQuette   *Christopher S. Hyatt, Ph.D.*

THE NATURE OF EVIL
From Aleister Crowley's Illustrated Goetia: Sexual Evocation
by Israel Regardie
New Falcon Publications, Eleventh Printing 2022

Lon Milo DuQuette and
Christopher S. Hyatt, Ph.D.
New Falcon Publications, Sixth Printing 2024

The purpose of this section is to stimulate, through metaphor and analogy, an understanding of Goetic operations and the concept of Evil. Through metaphor, we can only paint a picture. The shapes and colors can only be realized through meditation on the metaphors and doing the work itself. There is no substitute for the latter, and, while many have not practices Goetic evocation as classically described, they have evoked "unawares," over and over again, the same powerful forces and demons which have both helped and hindered them.

Like many of you I have "made up" my own rituals and have given my own names to these forces. At times I have given them proper names such as John, my neighbor, when his T.V. is too loud. At other times I have called these forces mother, friend, the system "It" or "me."

Sometimes I have benefited from "calling" these "Names" and sometimes I have suffered. Yet, neither benefit nor pain has caused me to reject the "howlings"[1] and simply

---

[1] "Goetia means 'howling'; but is the technical word employed to cover all the operations of that Magick which deals with gross, malignant or unenlightened forces." –Aleister Crowley

seek the comfort of "High Magick" alone. If I stand for anything, it is the acceptance of everything, (except, perhaps, for the hypocrisy demonstrated by many magicians and mystics who seek the light by running away from darkness).

Goetia is sometimes thought of as a wild card, sometimes that can get out of control, something which expresses the operator's lower desire to control others and improve his own personal life. And in fact this potential loss of control, this danger, the desire for self improvement and greater power is exactly what attracts many people to Goetia while horrifying and repelling others. Many label Goetia as simply evil.

Finding evil is an easy job. Just look at your friend, wife, husband, mother, father or for that matter the "guy" next door. The practice of Goetia is that other guy, sometimes dark, mysterious and powerful, something which tells the world that you are interested in yourself, interested in mastery as well as surrender (see Chapter Two in *Sex Magick, Tantra and Tarot: The Way of the Secret Lover*, New Falcon Publications, 1996 for an explanation of surrender and mastery).

Those who have disowned themselves and fear themselves often consider Goetic practices to be evil of the worst kind. Goetia is often thought of as an invitation to madness, the releasing of devouring and frightful forces. What Goetia is–is releasing of yourself from your own fears and illusions by direct confrontation. Goetic evocation is an invitation to flirt with the ambiguous relationship of "mind" and "matter." Remember, no one knows the true nature or actions of either and thus all arguments as to the "reality" of Goetic spirits are speculative and open to revision.

The question remains: What is evil? Some experts believe it is the intentional doing of harm without redemption. While this definition might provide these experts with a sense of comfort it provides me with little. It is too easy to play with words and ideas. For example according to this definition, Hitler might not be considered evil since some people believe that without his persecution of the Jews, Israel would not have been founded in the late forties. There is always some "good" which our "cause" and "order" crazed mind can find to rationalize or justify a horrible or unfortunate event.

Evil is an "externalization" and "objectification" of something fearful, horrifying, or different. Even can be label for something as simple as a person or an object that frustrates us. Evil is pain. Evil is the enemy. Evil is the Gods of other men. Evil is the night terrors. Evil is the overwhelming feeling of falling apart. Yet all these things are non-sense. Evil like other ideas exists because we as human exist. Nature knows not Evil, neither Good, nor for that matter Law. These are creations of the human mind, "explanations" which help us quiet the "terrors of the night." The human mind requires the belief in "its" idea of "order" for the sole purposes of the human mind. Thus the nature of evil is the human mind.

Each of us are full of doubts, frustrations, fears and anxieties. These demons of the soul are the hidden parts of our self. They are the disowned self, much like Goetia is the often disowned part of Magick. We normally don't present our dark side to others. Rarely, will anyone tell you their weak points let alone their deepest concerns. It is much easier and frequently less painful to find darkness outside of oneself.

What I present to the world, or for that matter what anyone presents, is at best a well-crafted ideal image, something desired, hoped for, something my brain and culture have helped create. Our mask is an illusion, a piece of the truth, a necessary one, but none the less only a piece of the truth.

CLINICAL PSYCHOLOGY AND GOETIA EVOCATION

Psychology, particularly therapeutic psychology, deals with people's fears and doubts. Psychologists label many of these fears as pathology. Psychologists have carefully followed in the footsteps of the Priest, who in his non-scientific but simple way labelled these things evil or demonic possession. *The average clinical psychologist is no more scientific than the priest.*

In the depths of the psychotherapeutic cave, the therapist assists the patient in evoking the rejected and hidden parts of his psyche. The greatest danger for the therapist, and for the patient, is the therapist's counter-transference. When this counter-tranference remains unconscious or gets "out of control," therapy becomes dangerous and ineffective. The complexes (demons) of both the therapist and the patient are mixing in an archaic cauldron. All sort of dangers are thought to be lurking. Sex becomes a strong possibility; so are violent outbreaks. Remember, these dangers are thought to be a result of the therapist's (the operator) losing control of the contents of his own unconscious processes, idealized fantasies, unfulfilled wishes and disowned attributes. Once this happens, it is believed that both the therapist and patient are adrift on a stormy sea in a sinking lifeboat.

The horrors and fears of counter-transference are so great that many State Laws explicitly prohibit "dual relationships" between therapist and patient; the therapist and patient must not become involved in relationships outside the safety of the therapeutic model. Dual relationships are thought of as a crossing of role boundaries between the therapist and patient. It is believed that the strict boundaries are necessary between the patient and therapist in order for the patient's cure. This is based on the theory that the patient's disease was caused by the breaking of proper boundaries in childhood.

The psychotherapeutic situation contains boundaries, strict ones set down by law, historical precedent, and theory.

The therapist becomes a mirror for the patient upon which the patient's highest aspirations and ideals as well as his disowned "shadowy" qualities can be projected. It is believed by some that he "working through" of both the "dark" and "ideal" illusions are fundamental to the patient seeing himself as well as others correctly, instead of the images and distorted fantasies originating and fixed in childhood.

The disappointment the patient feels when his illusions are crushed can be overwhelming. When his illusions of the therapist are crushed, his own self-illusions are threatened. The patient is both angry and depressed. If the therapist is a good "operator," he knows how to help the patient "crush" his illusions. He helps the patient free himself from the projections and splits. He knows how to help the patient realize that the therapist has both "good" and "bad" qualities and that these diverse qualities can reside in the same person at the same time. The therapist does not have to be worshipped or rejected. Either/or is the disease. Once the patient realizes this, he also "knows" that the same truth applies to himself. He is neither his ideal nor his darkness. These obvious realizations, however, cannot occur in a cool and objective way; for resolution to occur it often manifests in the heat, and sometimes exhaustion, of intense emotion. Power and force are necessary, and whether this manifests in extreme feeling or behavior or simply in moods and "neurotic" tests matters little. It matters only that they must manifest themselves, and the operator, by the definition of the situation, must stimulate them and in some way control them. He often stimulates them by breaking a taboo either in fact or by implication. He often teases and bribes the patient to be "naughty."

Sometimes the patient is the operator and the therapist is the receiver. In fact, these roles change, but not in a simple way. The therapist sometimes is "blank"–just receiving from the patient. At other times, the therapist is "active" while the patient receives images and conveys them back to the therapist in disguised forms.

What you have just read may sound contradictory: strict boundaries, deliberate violations of boundaries, the situation itself eliciting tests of boundaries, firm boundaries, fluid boundaries. In some sense it all sounds quite "crazy": projection, illusion, reality, boundaries, violations of trust freeing a person from the prison of his soul. Yet while sounding strange and often unscientific, if performed properly the desired results can occur. And what again are the desired results? One person helping another achieve what he most desperately wants and at the same time most desperately fears: control over his own life, freedom from devastating and repetitive illusions, freedom from reliving the past over and over again in the present. Real therapy teaches the patient how to embrace the whole of life, rejecting nothing, seeing the limitations of his ideals as well as the utility of his weaknesses. Real therapy teaches the art of violation, the breaking of taboos, opening the gates of both heaven and hell. Real therapy teaches style.

Taboos

Boundaries can be thought of as taboos. (See Taboo: *Sex, Religion and Magic*, New Falcon Publications, 2000.) Taboos are acts, places and things which no one, except maybe the priest, can touch without punishment. Taboos are "dirty." People who break taboos are thought of as dirty, evil people.

Yet, in our society is it not the "dirty" the dark which attracts attention? The garbage collector is highly paid for removing the leftovers of living. The bank clerk who handles hundreds of thousands of "dirty" dollars is paid less than the garbage collector. What is the nature of dirt, the common, which at the same time is valued and despised by so many? Money can do the bidding of anyone who has it. Money itself is only a shared illusion. It has no value except what people give it and it has no power except by what people do with it. The fluidity, malleability and indifference of money gives it a power unlike almost any other power in the world. Money sets boundaries and destroys them. Money itself doesn't care. And in this sense money is similar to the Goetia demons. They will work for anyone who knows how to use them. This is one of the horrors people attribute to Goetic workings. You "don't have to be respectable" for Goetia to work for you. Unlike other magical workings there is no implication that the operator has to be "good" and "holy" to achieve results. This idea in itself violates our model of "right" and "wrong", "just" and "unjust." In the Goetic world like in the real world the "bad" can and do prosper. Thus our belief in the moral order of the Universe appears violated by the simple existence of Spirits who will do the bidding of anyone.

Goetic evocation is the rejected "less respectable" side of magick. It is the work of the garbage collector. But it is also the most intimate side of the magick. It teaches the establishment of boundaries, of testing, of bribing, of lying and deceit. It provides the operator and the receiver with visions, suggestions and insights. It actualizes the hidden, the dark, the greedy, the needy, the powerful and the beautiful.

Goetic evocation can be very disappointing, sometimes

even horrifying, but it can never be boring. Unlike a child who determines the value of its knowledge by the approval or disapproval of a "higher authority" we learn the value of our Goetic work by the success or failure of our own work. Goetic Spirits are *not* the master of the magician but his servant. We do not rely on the "Spirits" per se to tell us that we did well. Goetia work is more "scientific" than other forms of magick in terms of our ability to measure its effects and, to some extent, replicate our results.

Goetic workings can also be potentiated by the use of hypnosis and sex. Trance and "exhaustion" resulting from sexual ecstasy are perfect methods for preparing the mind to receive more meaningful and powerful information.

In this book on Goetia, we have provided the student with a simple to use text on how to begin and become expert at Goetia evocation. We have included images of the Goetia Spirits, not to limit the student, but to stimulate his or her imagination. We have organized the text in such a way that the student doesn't have to flip through dozens of pages to find what he wants or needs.

Equally important, we have provided a technique for the sexual working of the Goetia Spirits. This is a powerful and sensual method. I have no doubt that some readers will be terrified and horrified at the potential power these techniques will release. We feel, however, that if you desire to practice magick you should practice it to its fullest. Safeguards have been provided, and the real dangers lie more in the mind than in the use of the methods.

Hypatia of Alexandria

DEVIL BE MY GOD

Lon Milo DuQuette

Author (or co-author) of the New Falcon Publication titles:
The Enochian World of Aleister Crowley: Enochian Sex Magic
Sex Magick, Tantra and Tarot: The Way of the Secret Lover
Aleister Crowley's Illustrated Goetia: Sexual Evocation

> "*I advise you to curb that waging tongue of yours.*"
> –Bishop of the Black Connons

> "*It's a habit I've never formed Your Grace.*"
> –Robin Hood

In A.D. 415 Cyril, the Bishop of Alexandria Egypt, found himself in a most awkward position. Not only was he burdened with the task of concocting viable doctrines[1] from the muddled and conflicting traditions of the young Christian cult, he was required to do so in the most sophisticated and enlightened pagan city on earth.

Long before the alleged virgin birth of the crucified savior, Alexandria, with her celebrated schools and library, nurtured the greatest minds of the Mediterranean world and Asia. Here, religion and philosophy were lovers, and their union gave rise to dynamic environment of dialog and debate. On more than one occasion Cyril tried to glean converts from the student body of the Neo-Platonic Academy, only to be stuck dumb by the discomforting realization that the fledgling philosophers

---

[1] Cyril is credited with formulating the concept of the Holy Trinity, an invention for which he was eventually canonized.

were far more knowledgeable than he about the subtleties and shortcomings of his own faith. Uncomfortable as he such moments were His Grace bore them dutifully. They afforded him the opportunity to suffer for his faith. His patience came to an end, however, when his faith and reputation were challenged by a brilliant and charismatic luminary of the Alexandrian School of Neo-Platonism, Hypatia–the greatest woman initiate of the ancient world.

Hypatia of Alexandria was without question the most respected and influential thinker of her day. The daughter of the great mathematician, Theon, she took over her father's honored position at the Academy and lectured there for many years. She, more than any other individual since Plotinus, the father of Neo-Platonism, grasped the profound potential of that school of thought. Her lectures were wildly popular and attracted a stream of scholars who was in Ne-Platonism the possibility of a truly universal spiritual order–a supreme philosophy–an enlightened religion to unite all religions. Such was the golden promise of Neo-Platonism, and Hypatia of Alexandria was its virgin prophetess.

Troubled by the continued degeneration of the Christian movement, its intolerance of other faiths and its dangerous preoccupation with miracles and wonders, Hypatia began a series of public lectures dealing with the cult. She revealed the pagan roots of the faith and systematically unmasked the absurdities and superstitions that had infected the movement. Then, with power and eloquence surpassing that of any Christian apologist, she elucidated upon what she understood to be the true spiritual treasures found in the purported teachings of the "Christ."

Her arguments were so persuasive that many new converts to the cult renounced their conversions and became disciples of Hapatia. Her lectures stimulated enormous interest in Christianity, but not Christianity as it was presented by Cyril, the Bishop of Alexandria.

Not blessed with the strength of character necessary to suffer a personal confrontation with Hypatia, Cryil embarked upon a campaign of personal vilification by preaching to his unwashed and fanatical flock that Hypatia was a menace to the faith, a sorceress in league with the Devil. These diatribes seemed to have little effect upon the sophisticated population of urban Alexandria who were beginning to realize that Bishop Cyril's Christianity was a cult that didn't play well with other children. Deep in the Nitrian dessert, however, Cyril's hateful words eventually reached the crude monastery of Peter the Reader.

Years of preaching to the wind and converting scorpions had uniquely qualified Peter to be the cleansing sword of the Prince of Peace, and the though of a devil-possessed woman attacking his savior was more than this man of God could stomach. Mustering a rag-tag collection of fellow hermits, he marched to Alexandria where they met with officials of the Caesarean church who informed him that each afternoon the shameless Hypatia drove her own chariot from the Academy to her home. Armed only with clubs, oyster shells, and the Grace of God, Peter and his mob ambushed Hypatia in the street near the Academy. Pulling her from her chariot they dragged her to her Caesarean church where they stripped her, beat her with clubs, and finally (because of an on-going debate over the soul's eternal status if the corpse remained whole) scraped the flesh from her bones with the oyster shells. The scoops of flesh and the rest of her remains were then carried away and burned.

The reaction of the Alexandrian community was one of confusion and shock, and the Neo-Platonist school was dealt a blow from which it never recovered. Although he went to great lengths to distance himself from the incident, Cyril took full advantage of the situation and used the terror of the moment to further intimidate the city and establish that the will of the Christian God was to be resisted at one's own risk.

The martyrdom of Hypatia was certainly not the first example of truth resisting evil and losing, but it did mark the beginning of a prolonged spiritual delirium tremor from which Western Civilization has never fully recovered. Even the bright souls who did not succumb to the universal madness were forced to blossom against the twisted projections of the collective nightmare.

Spiritual growth is not impossible in such an environment. But where wisdom is perceived by the world to be ignorance; love is considered sin, and all that is best in the human spirit is condemned and repressed, the road by which a seeker of enlightenment must travel takes many curious turns. On such a journey one's companions are outlaws and rebels; sacredness breeds in blaspheme, truth falls from the lips of false prophets, heaven is sought in hell, and God is the Devil himself.

BREAKING TRANCE

Steven Heller, Ph.D.

Author of the New Falcon Publication title:
*Monsters and Magical Sticks:
There's No Such Thing As Hypnosis?*

How do you know when you're getting too close to a fire? Of course, by feeling the heat! But what if you were unable to feel the heat? You would probably not know until you were burning yourself or you smelled your flesh burning. So many people go through life in such a deep trance, that they do not know when they are heading for trouble until they have stepped into it. They no longer know what they feel, want or need!

A small child hears his/her parents fighting and becomes afraid. They tell conflicting stories and she/he becomes confused. They send out incongruent messages and the anxiety rises to painful levels. One day she/he discovers that by "dropping out" and going off into inner-space-out, everything is better... for a while. If I can't feel it, hear it or see it, it can't get me. TRANCE IS BORN! Of course, if a truck is coming at you and you respond by "Not seeing or hearing it" I guarantee that you will feel it. Your trance will simply prevent you from getting out of the way.

A child enters a new and exciting world called school. S/he is curious and open to learning. "Children, we must all sit just like this and always raise your hand and there is one right way to do things and of course only one right answer!" says the adult called teacher. Day in and day out s/he sees things but is told they don't really exist. S/he feels things and is told that the feelings are not real and s/he doesn't really know what s/he feels in the first place. The secret of survival? Go into a trance! The result...years later s/he doesn't feel what there is to feel, can't hear what there is to hear and can't see what needs to be seen. Frustration, failure and pain is a constant companion.

The secret...*BREAK TRANCE!* You must learn to question and question some more. You cannot trust what you have been tranced into seeing, hearing, or feeling. Tonight, when you go to sleep, sleep on the other side of the be; sit at a different seat at meal times. For the adventurous, eat with your left hand (or right hand if you are left-handed). Read a book...from the last page; record conversations with those you have the poorest communication with. Look for problem area instead of avoiding them and then come up with three of the most unusual methods for solving the problem. Put a rubber band on your wrist and snap it when ever you feel yourself "dropping out."

Learn to talk to those parts of you that know the difference between trance and what is happening around you. For example, imagine that you begin to feel anxiety. Ask your inner guide to change the feeling into a picture; first a picture of what the feeling itself looks like, and then ask that part to change the picture into one that will help you discover what is really happening for (or to) you. Learn to hear the sound of colors and feelings and to see the feelings and sounds. In short, shake up your systems and break your patterns. (For many interesting and provocative methods of breaking trance, you might even purchase my book, *Monsters and Magical Sticks: There's No Such Thing As Hypnosis*.) Last, but not least, find a good hypnotist who will help you to use hypnosis and trance in order to end your hypnotic trance.

THE BLACK ART OF PSYCHOTHERAPY
Dr. Jack S. Willis

The multi entendre of the title is intentional and appropriate (multi: more than double, less than many). Let us count the ways.

First, psychotherapy is an art. It is not a science (the human-beings-are-laboratory-rats mentality of the behaviorists notwithstanding). A friend of mine, a philosopher of esthetics, defines art as: anything that people treat as art. So it is with psychotherapy. Any mad school that springs up and that gets people to call it "psychotherapy" then becomes a "psychotherapy." But is it good psychotherapy or just mad? We will return to that.

Second of the entendre is that, by whatever definition, it is a black art. And, in two ways. First, it supposedly deals with the dark side of the person. Call it dark, call it hidden, call it black; by whatever name, it is the devil within us that is awakened in psychotherapy. Second, as an art, it is dependent not only on the artistry of the practitioner, but also on the (en)light(enment) of the therapist. We will return to that, too.

Third of the entendre, it is a black art because, examined closely, it employs the same techniques, albeit in different robes, as does thaumaturgy and invocation of the spirits. The names of the spirits are different, and the drugs are (usually) different, and the invocation rituals are different; but it is magic nonetheless. And black magic at that.

Do you wish to move to a different plane of consciousness? Try hypnosis or alpha wave biofeedback or sodium amytal or any number of emotion altering drugs. Do you wish to feel fully? Try Gestalt or psycho-drama or Primal. Do you wish to probe the unknown and unknowable. Try Jungian. Do you wish a re-birth? Try Rankian, or rebirthing, or age regression (even to rebirth in former lives). Do you wish to be loved? Try Rogerian. Is death your issue? Existentialist therapy awaits. Or, perhaps you want better sex or mind-body unity? Try Reichian, Bio-energetics, Feldenkrais, Rolf or Alexander technique. For every passion there is a therapy, and for every therapy there is a passionate following. What to do? What to do? We will return to that, too. There is an answer.

Final of the entendre, it is also an art of the patient (really a student rather than a patient). The art of the student is where we will finish our exploration.

Psychotherapy As Art

No two people are alike. A photograph as art can be duplicated an infinite number of times. Similarly an etching. A bronze can be recast. But people are ever unique and ever changing. The interchange between therapist and student is a ballet. Is there a leader and a follower? The can be; there doesn't have to be. But one thing of this dance is certain: if the therapist can only dance to his own tune, if he is committed to a school and a technique irrespective of the student, then the ballet will be an awkward and even disastrous performance.

How then does the student choose a teacher? How can you judge your teachers artistic sensibility? I will answer the choice of teacher question here and wait until later to address the question of his artistry. The answer to choosing a teacher is easy, if not obvious. There are two questions to ask: (1) what is your objective and (2) what is your time line. Put it this way: if you exercise, do you want a little workout once or twice a week or do you want to really tone your muscles? Do you want to exercise until you lose 10 pounds, or do you want to make it a part of your life? What is your objective and what is your time line? If your objective is limited and/or you want quick answers, then choose a teacher whose method is quick and direct. Rational emotive therapy, hypnosis, cognitive-behavioral or behaviorism are good answers.

If your objective is to increase your happiness quotient, to correct your errors in living, to exercise the daemons inside you, then choose a teacher who increases anxiety. If your teacher promises to love you unconditionally, run. If your teacher tells you that he is problem oriented, run. If your teacher tells you that he will deal with your emotions but not with your thinking, run. If he says he deals with the here-and-now not with the past, sprint. If he says he is only a (fill in the school) therapist and that is the only school he believes in, find a new teacher. There is no sense in finding a teacher of French when you are planning a trip to Germany.

But, since nothing in life is easy, if he says he is totally flexible, that he is eclectic, that he uses whatever is appropriate with no commitment to any theory, then make a mad dash. In psychotherapy, the word eclectic is often a synonym "for I don't know what I am doing, I just do whatever feels right."

If your objective is long-term personal growth, then choose the teacher whose statement to you make you anxious, unsettled, nervous, unsure. Therein lies an answer.

The Dark Side of Our Soul

I will make the, I think very reasonable, assumption that anyone who reads this book is interested in maximizing their potential and increasing their productivity and creativity. For such a person therapy is a Godsend (to steal a metaphor). My teacher, Israel Regardie (and Dr. Hyatt) said that he would not teach anyone the methods of the Golden Dawn unless they had had at least 4 years of Reichian therapy. Regardie took that position for a very good reason. Until we have removed some of the darkness within our own soul, any attempt at thaumaturgy will only evoke our own indwelling devils. Freud said that repression and sublimation were necessary for one to live in the society. Reich claimed the only answer was to change society. I am less pessimistic then those two towering figures.

When they were writing, we did not have the knowledge of the developmental steps of the ego and we did not have the work of Piaget on children's cognitive development. I've proven it enough times to enough students; that I can say with some confidence that the main issue in our personal psychology is mistakes in thinking. As children we attempted to understand the silly (sometimes crazy, sometimes evil) statement and actions of our parents. However, children and adults live in different worlds of knowledge and thinking. What seems obvious to a parent, is adult babble to a child. Parents pretend that they are teaching the child to…(behave, to considerate, share, be polite, etc.) when in truth all they are doing is confusing the child. The child tries to make sense out of the teaching, misunderstands most of what is taught; and neither the child nor the parent knows how off the two are.[1]

Human beings are magnificent but flawed creatures. We take the mistakes of childhood, we live them our whole life, we never recognize they were wrong to begin with, and that they are now doubly wrong as adults. Thus we live our lives in war with ourselves. It is a terrible waste of energy. We take

---

[1] My favorite story is the mother who yells at her child to not play with the lamp because he will break it. A moment later, and CRASH! So, "I told you not to play with the lamp, now look what you've done!" But, says the bright child, "I wasn't playing with the lamp, I was playing with the spaceship." Children live in different cognitive universes than do adults.

the glory and the beauty of the infant and create anger and misery of the adult. It is to take a David of Michelangelo and re-sculpt him into a Henry Moore burdened and struggling tortured soul.

It doesn't need to be, it shouldn't be. Freud said, where the id was, there the ego shall be. I would say where darkness was there light shall be.

The (En)Light(enment) Of The Therapist

There is a danger in psychotherapy. The danger is called the therapist. The therapist is the magician of this black art. When he attempts to exorcise your devils is he doing it by inserting his own? In psychological terms, is he attempting to project his own devils into you? And how can you tell if he is?

There is no infallible answer to this one. There are some guides. How much therapy has your proposed therapist had (minimum of 7 years)? What kind of therapy(ies) did he have? Is he attempting to use a particular school of therapy in which he has not himself been a patient If so, choose another teacher. You can ignore licenses and degrees. They mean nothing. What matters is the knowledge of and therapy experience of your proposed therapist, not what degrees or licenses he does or does not have. In how many schools of therapy is he knowledgeable? The minimum is two. But here is the most important rule of all: if the therapist talks about himself (other than to answer your questions) or he frequently brings in how he feels or would feel in your situation then he is definitely trying to work out his own problems on your time. You have come upon a dark soul (irrespective of or in spite of any therapy he may have had). Stop now. You are with the wrong teacher. Darkness cannot create lightness of being.

Choosing A Therapist

It may seem like I have talked of little else. But the subject is not exhausted. As a Reichian therapist of nearly 30 years experience, there is more that can be added. As you may know, Reichian therapy is a body approach to therapy. Therefore, we get a lot of information from the physical appearance, the gestures, the voice tone, the eyes, etc. Here, then, are some tips from the Reichian couch. Your therapist should have forehead creases. The should not be permanent (a furrowed brow), they should become prominent when the eyebrows are raised and, except or the crease, disappear when the eyebrows are lowered. His eyes should be clear, very focused, and they should move easily. There should be a definite nasal-labial line (the line from the corner of the nose to the corner of the mouth). The neck muscles should not be prominent. The voice should be resonant, coming firm an open throat rather than a constricted one. If he takes a big breath, both the belly and the chest should move. Of the things I have listed here, the most important is the forehead and the eyes. If his eyes are dull or they do not move easily or his forehead has no crease lines or has permanent creases, quit now. What if you have been making wonderful progress with just this kind of therapist? My suggestion: take a six-month vacation from this therapist and look into some others. The vacation will be good for you anyway and the experience of some visits to other teachers might give you some perspective on his virtues and his failings.

If you have not chosen a therapist, or if you are going to take a vacation, here is my suggestion: There are four good schools of depth therapy: psychodynamic, ego psychology (also called object relations), neo-Freudian, and Reichian. Note that the word is *psychodynamic*, not *psychoanalysis*. The foundation is the same, but the technique is very different.

Notwithstanding that Jungian is very popular among the readers of New Falcon Publications, I would urge against it. I have yet to see good results emerge from Jungian analysis. Stay as far away as possible from Primal therapy or any variant. Adlerian, in the right hands, is an acceptable alternative; but then go to someone else afterwards to get to the areas that Adlerian can not address. Bio-energetics is not bad except that you walk around angry for years, in the process losing marriages, jobs, and friends. Existential therapy can be done well, but it is rare. Most therapists proclaiming themselves as existentialist have not done the study necessary to make good use of the art. Existentialist is not one school; it is a whole bunch with differing degrees of worth. Of all the rest, I would say: Ignore them. They are not depth therapy, and they can not do the job you deserve.

The Art Of The Patient

Now, finally, to the most important part: **YOU!** Even a truly good teacher is no good if the student will not study, if the student will not do his homework. If you are not important to your self why should you be important to your therapist? Is it rational to expect that your therapist will work hard for you when you will not work hard for yourself?

Here is a statement that you have probably never heard any therapist make: the two most important qualities that you need to bring to the study are *anger* and *courage*. Anger in the form of the demand of yourself, the commitment, that you will not settle for less than you can be. You will not settle for injuring your children because you have not uncovered your own daemons. You will not settle for less productivity, less creativity, less enjoyment of the wonder of life than is possible for you to achieve. That does not mean that your goal is perfection. We leave that realm to the Gods. It does mean that however much you can uncover, understand, and correct is the minimum you will settle for and the devil take the hindmost.

Then there is courage. Daemons are scary creatures. What are your daemons? Are they depression, anxiety, anger, guilt, facing the fact that your parents are not the nice people you want them to be, realizing that you have been living your life for other people and not for yourself, realizing that you are not as important as you want to think you are, realizing that you made a bad choice in a mate, realizing that you have been pretending to enjoy sex? For all your determination to surrender the darkness for the light, you have to have the courage to stay the course, confess the big and the little, accept that you are what you are–not what you want to be, and most of all: the determination to accept that the losses of your childhood are permanent losses. That last one is a biggie and it raises another factor.

Intellectual integrity should be another part of your art. A man of intellectual integrity does not attempt to fake reality. *What is, simply is*. It is not subject to our fantasies, our wishes, or our ideals. It is not pretty or ugly. It is not noble or ignoble. It is not heroic or cowardly. It simply is. As honesty is telling the truth to others, so integrity is telling the truth to ourselves. It is much harder. We know when we are lying to someone else. *But the lies we tell our self are the lies we live by.* They are part of our very being. And they are corrosive.

There is much that could be said here, but there is only one thing I want to add. Never accept anything your therapist says except as a possibility to *honestly examine*. Your own mind is the ultimate judge of the validity of any idea or interpretation. Yes, you are student to this teacher because you can not uncover your own errors of thinking. But the alternative is not to turn your mind over to someone else.

Your therapist may or may not be an advanced soul, an enlightened person. He may have penetrating insights, and he may be "a wise man" (as the Talmudists would say). And, certainly, you are in his office to take a graduate degree in living. Certainly his explanations and interpretations deserve a respectful audience. But, in the end, it is our trained judgment that is the authority. Your therapist can demand all he wants that he is right because he is the therapist/authority. Do not buy it. On the subject of you, you are the authority. Take every idea he puts forth, examine it with anger, courage, and integrity, and then, if it is wrong, discard it. Your life is a temple. It deserves respect, reverence, and prayer; don't let it go to waste, it is too sacred.

ANOTHER BEDTIME STORY
Dr. William S. Hyatt, Ph.D.

Our story starts in the living room of Sam Simple, a carpet salesman who is twenty-nine-years-old. Sam lives with his wife Tammy in the last stronghold of racism and muddle-dum-Burbank, California.

When Sam and Tammy first met-three years ago at a dance club in Hollywood-they fell in "love at first sight." The romantic couple quickly moved in together and soon after, married. While the romance was brewing, Sam continually assured himself and his friends that his relationships with them would not change. He would not stop being independent, he would not forget his old pals, he would not spend all of his time with his new wife. Of course, Sam did forget his friends, he did forget his autonomy, and he did forget his promises.

Although Sam told me that he really loved Tammy, and that she was "perfect," I wondered what sort of powerful drug he had taken which made him lose sight of reality and forget all of the promises that he had made.

As Sam and Tammy's relationship grew, so did Sam's Visa bill. They bought new furniture-antiques, because they hold their value, was the rationalization that I was given. New clothes, actually "vintage clothes;' a new term coined by people who sell old clothes. And they both started hobbies, collecting various types of bric-a-brac. These items were bought because Sam and Tammy wanted to show their friends that they were different, and of course superior. They bought new cars, or old cars that had been fixed up to look "perfect." They did make one strange concession to the future, they moved into a new– yes, a brand new-apartment complex; one which had no previous smells in the carpet.

In the new apartment the young couple had found a home. They started decorating. First they put up lace curtains (from Wards). Then they bought towels to match their toilet seat cover. Soon they bought antique furniture. An old free-standing radio that didn't work very well, but was very pretty. Sam bought old phones, from the 1930s. These phones also didn't work very well. They were hard to dial, hard to use and bulky, but again, they conveyed the uniqueness of Sam and Tammy's existence.

As the young couple started to put their scent everywhere in the house, they felt more and more at home. Tammy started collecting 1930s sheet music, which she framed and hung above the old radio, and soon Sam bought an old Victrola, which when played sounded like a dozen cats getting mauled by a starving pit bull.

As the couple added more and more "things" to their home, they became more and more unhappy. Were these possessions a mere substitute for the empty feelings in their lives? Sam started changing jobs, as did Tammy. They both started eating health food and taking more than fifty vitamins each, every day. Tammy sold her car and bought a new Ford, while Sam had his vintage VW bug repainted. Sam sold his 1930s fully restored wristwatch in favor of a new Timex. When the Timex broke, he bought a 1960s Omega, gold-tone.

Sam and Tammy were through nest building, they had filled their nest with many toys and were looking at Visa payments, rent and auto expenses that took ninety percent of their combined net incomes. Should they start a family or start a hobby?

Although Sam "forgot" about his previous promises to himself and his friends, he did take a firm stand on one conviction: "I hate kids and will not have them:' Although Tammy verbally went along with this mandate, she even said that she was incapable of having kids, she secretly wanted to fill her nest. Would the remaining ten percent of the couple's income support the next generation of nest-builders and antique collectors?

When Sam arrived home from work one day, he was surprised to find a note from "mom," aka Tammy. It said, "I am at doctor Rothenberg's office, will be back by five." As Sam sat around and wondered what sort of ailment befell his simple wife, he started to grind his teeth. When Tammy walked in the front door, she exclaimed that she was pregnant, as if no one on earth had ever been pregnant before. But, she was more than pregnant–somehow she had been transformed. She had a look in her eyes, a look that said: "I am a mother in training, now I am an expert."

Sam went crazy. His teeth stopped grinding. He broke pictures, vases, records and even broke a blood vessel. He knew that he must take a stand. He had lied to himself about everything since he had been married, and he knew that he couldn't tolerate this major breech of conduct on the part of his wife. He told Tammy that if she wanted to have the baby fine, but that he would leave within the hour. Otherwise, she should turn right back around, and ask Dr. Rothenberg to perform an abortion, immediately.

When Tammy left the house crying, Sam was alone in his living room.

He stood staring at his mannequins dressed in World War I German military uniforms. These mannequins had become his children. They didn't eat or talk back. They didn't require time, unless one wanted to give it, and best of all they were UNIQUE-like Sam.

The one on the right side of the room was dressed in a blue enlisted man's dress uniform, with a red sash across his chest. The brass buttons were shined every week, as were the many medals. The white pants were starched and pressed and the long sword hung powerfully to the right side. The highlight of the outfit was the spiked helmet, which was on the mannequin's head. The helmet was a shiny black shell with an impressive brass plate of an eagle clutching a saber adorning its front. The tall and glossy spike rose smartly above the helmet. This spike might be the esoteric German phallic symbol, in the form of a six inch pointed spike, rising out of someone's hand. The left side of the room contained a life-size statue of the Jack-in-the-Box. He was also dressed in a German spiked helmet, although he was lacking the matching uniform. Covering the walls were pictures of German soldiers in ancient battles. Prussians firing old cannons at helpless natives, and a framed picture of Himmler, with the following caption: "A great man, one who served his country and followed orders, no matter how much he personally opposed them." Was Himmler an earlier version of Oliver North?

As Sam sat and thought of his life, he wondered if a child meant he would have to give up his precious collection of German/Prussian artifacts. He decided that it did, a thought he couldn't stand. "The baby would have to sleep in this room. It would cry all night long. And most importantly, I would have to sell all of my toys to keep it in diapers."

He hoped that Tammy would make the right decision. When she came home in tears, all Sam could think of was his collection of military relics: "Did you do it?" He gasped. When she started crying again, he knew that she had, and he was relieved. Now he could keep buying his junk/toys and more importantly-he could tell his friends that he stood up for his rights: "I told her what to do, and she ain't going to have no kid in my house."'

The next week Sam made a visit to his doctor. That night he told his wife that he had made a statement of his individuality, "I got myself fixed:' Now when Tammy talks to Sam about planning for the future, children are never discussed, instead they talk about new uniforms, sheet music, old cars and a bigger nest. And, Sam has again shown how unique he really is.

The scene now moves to Pasadena California. We move into the lives of Melvin and Dodie Weiss, another couple recently married. They too are unique, but in a different way.

Melvin is an elitist, like Sam, although he is an intellectual one. His young wife Dodie, nineteen-years-old, thinks that everyone is equal...she isn't very bright. Dodie looks a bit like a bowling ball. She is four-foot-ten in height, while weighing about one hundred forty-eight pounds. She has typical Jewish features, highlighted by ugly frizzy hair, which is closely cropped and covered with a light dandruffy frost. The many birth marks which adorn her face look like a map of war-torn Europe. Like Tammy, Dodie wears old clothes, but she buys them at the Goodwill, as it is the only place she can afford to shop. Also like the Simples, the Weisses have a lot of old junk, but not by choice; they simply can't afford new junk yet.

Melvin doesn't love or respect his wife, but she is eighteen years younger than him, and very fertile. Melvin hypothesizes that his wife thinks all people are equal because she is a moron, and because she looks like a bowling ball. He doesn't mind Dodie's looks, as he is no better looking himself. In fact, he looks a bit like a bowling pin. Melvin is tall, with wide hips and no visible hair on his arms or legs. His face seems to lack features, unless you strain to find his dull eyelids. Melvin and Dodie, they seem to be a happy and well matched couple.

Dodie, a natural Jew, has many important opinions to share. Although Melvin tells her that opinions are like assholes, everyone has them, ultimately he agrees with everything that her small mind can conjure up; he does this since he can't seem to convince her to accept any of his views. Either they are too complex or she is too narrow in her world view. The first opinion she tells her new husband, is they must plan for their future. They should buy grave plots at Mount Sinai, so that they can be together forever, or at least until some developer builds condos on the property. Next, Dodie convinces Melvin that he should work two jobs so that they can make payments on their land, and send her to school at the same time. Meanwhile, they live in a seedy, roach-filled apartment in the ghetto of Pasadena. Melvin drives an ancient VW bug that always starts, but that has no heat, windows or padding in the seats. While Dodie takes the bus all over the Los Angeles area.

While Dodie and Melvin are struggling as students and planning for their future, they continually reassure each other that they are unique. They certainly are a perfect match, after all bowling pins and bowling balls often go together.

Dodie tells anyone who will listen that she doesn't value material things (is this because she doesn't have any?) but only her husband and future family. She tells anyone who will listen that when she graduates she will go to work as a teacher, forgetting the fact that she has been fired from twelve jobs in the last eighteen months. Dodie's plans continue: when the family has a double income, they will move to the mountains and buy a piece of land, (no, not another grave plot) so that they can build their dream box; no, I mean house. This dream house will enable the youngsters to raise a family and be secure, safe and trapped.

Although Melvin feels that his grave plot and his dream house are somehow closely related, he can't figure out how. He is very busy working three jobs now, so he isn't able to understand that he has become a tool for his wife's whims.

Dodie wants to surround herself with clutter and junk, although not the kind that Sam and Tammy have, the kind that cries in the night. Soon, she will be able to justify everything that she does, including the following of her whims, for the sake of her children. She will surround herself with activities, such as knitting groups, women's groups and co-op babysitting groups. She will pretend that all of her friends are equal to her, while she secretly judges them, thereby making herself feel superior. Most uniquely, Dodie will become an instant expert on child rearing. She will tell her weak-willed husband that they will raise their children differently, better, wiser and with better results. She will tell him of all of her plans for accomplishing these goals, and how brilliant they are.

Although Melvin will try to leave Dodie before they get to the reproduction scene, he will soon come back to her, as he won't be able to make it on his own; without his "mommy" to make his plans. In turn, Dodie will have a nervous breakdown, as she worries that she has not been fertilized yet. She secretly wonders if she can find any other man dumb enough to nest with her. After all, her plans are very unique.

The earth is a giant egg. It is waiting to be fertilized again. Who will do it? Sam, a man for all seasons, who lives in the past, as a way of avoiding the future. Or will Melvin, a man who understands the secrets of the universe. Melvin knows that everything is related to either the crack in someone's ass or the crack in the cosmic egg, but he can't figure out which one is more correct.

Should we get a diaper for the planet or for the people on the planet? Should we get a diaper for the unborn eggs or should we re-fertilize again? Should we collect war relics or start new wars? Should we believe that we are unique or should we attempt to understand language limitations? Should we build new nests in the mountains or should we build future nests in the cemetery? Should we go to college or should we sell carpet? Should we buy new cars or drive old ones? Should we paint our old cars and call them classic or should we leave them alone and call them junk? Should we marry bowling balls or marry bowling pins? Finally, should we delude ourselves with whims, fantasy and societal customs or should we find a new egg to inhabit and new lives to fertilize?

What we can learn from the true tale of Sam/Tammy and Melvin/Dodie, is that people attempt to place themselves in an illusory place of uniqueness and self-importance. Further, this is done primarily through the misuse of language. Language is the prisoner, the jailer, the warden and the cell. Language is also the crime. With language we delude ourselves, delude others and build a false wall of illusion around our lives and actions. Because Sam calls his VW or his clothes vintage, they are better than Melvin's who has a junk VW (same year-1963) and old clothes. Who is superior? Who is more unique? The very notion of distinguishing the difference between the two and judging which is superior is ludicrous. In fact, the notion of superiority and uniqueness is just another example of limiting language.

ECSTACY

Dr. Israel Regardie

[NOTE: This is the fifth chapter from Dr. Israel Regardie's book Healing Energy, Prayer, & Relaxation *(New Falcon Publications). Written later in his life, this book distills the knowledge he accumulated throughout a life of devoted study and practice in Magic, Natural Healing, and Psychology.*

An attitude of cold objectivity and lack of feeling during prayer is, so far as my understanding goes, quite impossible. I cannot conceive how a person who has pondered over the 23rd Psalm, for example, and understood it to the extent of employing it as their private and personal metaphysical treatment, can refrain from being moved emotionally. For a prayer to be successful it should have the effect of bringing about an inner crisis. Eventually it should induce a vigorous emotional reaction that, when understood and controlled and directed, can wing the soul towards the realization of the presence of God, the goal that is ever sought after. A real ecstasy should result, a thoroughgoing standing out of the mind from itself and all its concerns with the body and its problems, from neurosis and inner turmoils. It should raise the individual above their personality, so as to realize their true divine nature. The whole secret of prayer lies in this direction. It aims at ecstatically moving the individual to transcend themselves. In short, prayer consists of a complex of psychological gestures designed to enable us to recover our true identity–which is God. In praying, we evolve to the stature of full and perfect adulthood, where we are able

Dr. Israel Regardie
One of the foremost authorities on the theory and practice of Magick.

"...a representative of the great 'occult tradition' of the late 19th century, whose major names include Madame Blavatsky, W.B. Yeats, MacGregor Mathers, A.E. Waite, Aleister Crowley and Dion Fortune. Even in such distinguished company, Regardie stands out as a figure of central importance."–Colin Wilson

to perceive our true and essential relationship to all that lives, and our entire dependence upon the One Mind in whom we do exist and have our being.

Not only is this an intellectual or mental achievement, but the realization itself becomes fired by the rapture that the meditation on prayer should arouse. As a successful operation, prayer must provide scope for man's every faculty. Thus conceived, it is the spiritual and emotional stimulus that is calculated to restore the sense of our original identity with Godhead. Or, at least, it will enable the individual to contact in some novel and dynamic way that boundless source of power and wisdom which we conceive of as God. It is no request to an impossible God for bounty or reward like a child asking presents of its mother or father. Sincerely undertaken, prayer should mobilize all the qualities of the self. Integrity is the essence and goal of its nature. The inner fervor it awakens should reinforce the whole individual, energizing the concept s/he holds in mind for treatment so it becomes realized as concrete reality. This inner fervor is the sine qua non of success.

Neville [Goddard] rightly surmises that to make one's prayers fulfill themselves one must go mad temporarily. Even as lovers become excited and moved by the fleeting thought of the sweetheart, so the one employing prayer should react also. They must be capable of becoming so enthused and spiritually excited by the prayer that the whole self lets go of itself and flies directly to its divine goal, as though impelled inexorably like an arrow from the bow of devotion and aspiration. Success in demonstration comes about not exclusively through human effort, but primarily because the divine force courses through one. First, however, one must have touched adequately the divine universal mind, and right rapture provides the drive towards that goal.

I have always questioned in my mind whether prayer of the quiet unemotional variety is of any ultimate value at all. This cold blooded petitioning finds no real place within the highest conceptions of spiritual achievement. An ancient mystic and metaphysician once wrote we should inflame ourselves with prayer. And here is the secret revealed in a single word. We must not, counsels Jesus, use vain repetitions as the heathens do. But we may repeat intelligently the prayer again and again until the meaning is driven home, firing us spontaneously to increased devotion.

In his fascinating book *The Psychology of Suggestion*, Dr. Boris Sidis made an observation which is particularly *apropos* and pertinent to this discussion. He remarks, "we know that a strange emotion narrows down the field of consciousness." In this way, therefore, suggestions are much more readily accepted by the subconscious mind, than were the mind extensive and preoccupied with a host of sensory perceptions and motor impulses. "We often find;' he continues, "that people under the emotion of intense excitement lose, so to say, their senses; their mind seems to be paralyzed, or rather, so to say, the one idea that produces the excitement banishes all other ideas, and a state of monoideism, or concentration of the consciousness is thus effected." Monoideism was the term employed by [Dr. James] Braid[1] to describe the hypnotic state, when the subject's attention, all plastic and pliable, could be turned to any one topic, and a total concentration of his mind on that single topic procured. It is for this reason, then, that emotional exaltation is so necessary to metaphysical technique, or to the practice of auto-suggestion, for then the mind's stream becomes automatically narrowed down to a single point, permitting the penetration of the suggestion.

We must pray so the whole being becomes aflame with a spiritual devotion, before which nothing can stand. In that intensity, we rediscover what we always have been in reality. All illusions and errors and limitations fade utterly away before this divine fervor. When the soul literally burns up–"as pants the heart for cooling stream," as the popular hymn goes–then spiritual identity with, or realization of, God becomes more than a possibility. "The desire of Thy house hath burnt me up." Then the heart's desire is accomplished without effort because actually it is God who prays and God who answers. There is none other to pray, and nothing that can be accomplished, save that for which God makes the gesture. The desire that is holy becomes fact-objective phenomenal fact for all to see.

Prayer is a dramatic gesture, implying the utmost in emotional capacity and in spiritual understanding. It bears no relationship to the infantile concept of asking favors of some

---

[1] Dr. James Braid was a Scottish surgeon, often considered the father of modern hypnosis.

father-like deity. It is, however, a gesture of realizing the divine reality that has never been obscured, save in the conscious mind. Unconsciously we have always known what we were and to what spiritual power we were related. That knowledge has never been entirely lost. By making gestures of the right and most intelligent kind, we regain a full and conscious realization of our own Godhead.

A study of ancient prayer techniques seems to yield the fact that former authorities, unlike so many today, were not averse to conceiving of prayer as a complex process of auto-suggestion. The so-called affirmations of modern metaphysics are quite obviously suggestions. One ancient prayer, or invocation, as once they were called, strongly and frequently employs in its structure the modern usage of "I am" affirmations. For example, it affirms as part of its rubric, "I am He the Bornless Spirit having sight in the feet, strong, and the immortal fire. I am He the Truth. I am He whose mouth ever flameth. I am He that lighteneth and thundereth. I am He from whom is the shower of the Life of Earth. I am He the Grace of the World."

This is the peroration of a long and complicated prayer filled with certain obscure and barbaric elements not altogether comprehensible to the modern mind. There is little doubt however but that the motivating trend of the preliminary parts of the prayer or invocation was gradually to excite the so-called conscious mind of the invoker until a high pitch of fervor was induced. It affirmed the relationship of man to God, narrating the great power and wisdom of God. The intention was that the mind at the critical moment, due to the extraordinary degree of excitement and ardor provoked, should be thrown into a state of high suggestibility. That ardent peak achieved, the peroration containing the potent suggestions was uttered, and the magical results were obtained because the suggestions were accepted and became effectual.

A state of high suggestibility is one during which the normal reticence of the mind to extraneous ideas, the endo-psychic resistance of which psychoanalysis speaks, is overcome. This overcoming of the resistance may not necessarily be a permanent conquest. But from the point of view of the prayer technique, that is a matter of very small moment. The resistance is abrogated for a sufficiently long period-a few seconds or a few minutes at most may be its duration—to permit of the immediate acceptance of the suggestions. Once in the mind's deeper structure, they can do their work effectively. From within they evoke various states of consciousness that are constantly present though dormant. They are rather like parental imagos present within the unconscious levels of the mind, remaining dormant until mobilized or reinforced by current events or people. The dormancy is overcome by the prayer, and these latent psychic states are stimulated sympathetically into dynamic activity by the suggestions. Suggestions by themselves mean nothing, and of themselves contribute nothing. They only render kinetic previous but unknown contents of the mind.

I am quite willing to admit calling this process suggestion or auto-suggestion does not in the least render explicable to our minds what we know to occur. A psychological phenomenon of extraordinary interest and power has occurred. We do not know what it really is, but we give it the name of suggestion. Merely to give a scientific term to an unknown process, however, does not necessarily explain it–though this seems to be a common trait of the modern scientific and critical mind. Nor do these terms tell us in what way suggestion works, nor the inner mechanism of its operation within the mind itself. But at least this may be said. The phenomena of suggestion to some extent can be experimentally induced–presuming that we have a good subject and a capable operator-and that goes a very long way for us. This is more than can be said of prayer in its formal religious or even metaphysical sense. I have never heard of any metaphysician who would be willing to "demonstrate" under test conditions. But this is exactly what can be done with suggestion and auto-suggestion. Very severe scientific conditions have been imposed upon experimenters, and these have been satisfactorily fulfilled. And though we do not know in the least the modus operandi of suggestion, yet a similar comment can be made upon prayer. We have not the least knowledge how prayer, when successful, operates and how it produces the amazing results which occasionally we do see. For the sake of convenience therefore, we could use the word suggestion and auto-suggestion possibly, in order to convey the same series of ideas as are involved in the idea of prayer.

Moreover, for the sake our own understanding, we can liken the process of successful evocation of inner states of consciousness by means of prayer, which overcomes resistance at the gates of the unconscious levels, by reference to Jungian analysis. The contemplation of dreams in the light of mythological and religio-philosophical processes, awakens out of their latency primordial archetypes that are residues of former cultural periods, to function anew within the conscious sphere. These residues are the psychological imprints, as it were, left by the efforts of former generations of men to solve satisfactorily their own inner and spiritual problems.

As we ourselves become confronted by difficulties of mind and emotion with which we do not know how to deal, the libido, or the mind's energy, under the stimulus of analysis slips away or regresses from the present time into the past. It regresses not merely to infancy, but to older and more ancient levels within the mind where are stored the phylogenetic results of man's age-old attempts adequately to fulfill ourselves and our spiritual aspirations. These historical records or primordial archetypes of the collective unconscious often assume in dreams the guise of magical processes of old, formerly celebrated religious rites, mythological worship and devotions paid to the old gods. These archetypes, layer by layer, become successively awakened by means of the analytical process. It is as though not merely the superficial aspects of the mind labored to deal with its problems, but every level, every faculty of the whole mind, the whole self, were enlisted in one prodigious effort. In his book The Integration of the Personality, Jung devotes a whole chapter to the analysis of numerous dreams of a single person, pointing out how the primordial archetypes were evoked into redemptive activity to bring about this desired process of integration, the achievement of wholeness, of perfection.

Possibly one great advantage of the psalms and ancient prayers or invocations lies in the fact that they awaken memories, not merely of infancy but of the far distant past. They bring us in touch once more with the unconscious self hidden deep in our own minds. Therefore, we impinge upon the whole collective background of our individual lives, upon the immeasurable past of duration when the instinctual forces–symbols of powers of miraculous potency and superior wisdom-flourished and prospered and functioned without the conscious interference that belongs to our present day and age. Through such usage of prayer, we recover the vitality and the involuntary higher guidance that obtains in the acquisition of the knowledge of our instincts. Moreover, and what is important for us, we obtain the sense of participating with and belonging to the whole rhythmic stream of life which pulses and vibrates in the world around us.

One of the most outstanding characteristics of primitive man was participation mystique, an anthropological term to denote that mystical sense of identification with nature, when trees and rivers and clouds, and every phenomenon soever, were alive and spoke. Nature was intelligent and peopled widely with dryads and hamadryads, with nymphs, fauns and centaurs. This, today, we would call the projection of unconscious images, the projection as on to an outer mirror of the world of what actually existed within. Primitive man projected their own primitive emotions upon all the objects of his or her world, and not understanding themselves within, the things their environment presented were similarly primitive and savage and terrifying. It was necessary, as evolution and development proceeded, to break up this participation mystique, so that in the rejection of unconscious image-projection the mind would divorce itself from nature and be enormously improved and enriched.

But we have gone too far. The swing of the pendulum has carried us to the opposite extreme. Now we are afraid to see any kind of intelligence in nature outside of our own. We have developed mind to the extent that we have lost sight of the seedling world of unconscious forces within. We have strayed from our roots, and we are lost and stranded with no real sense of direction or guidance. The mind that we evolved has turned out to be, by itself, an empty bubble. Chained to the rock of our own isolation like Prometheus, the vultures gnaw at our vitals. Our own intellectual progress is the very thing that now destroys us.

We are obliged to go forward, to press onwards to the unknown future, not merely to retrace regressively our footsteps to the forgotten past. What we have gained so laboriously in these many centuries of evolution we cannot sacrifice without deliberation, not even for God. And we cannot conceive that God would demand such abrogation of ourselves. That indeed

would be disastrous and catastrophic. We would be untrue to our birthright. Instead, we must bring the past up-to-date, as it were. We must recover the former sense of our divine kinship with nature, with things, with men. Then we can press forward, taking with us what we have formerly gained from nature by dint of heroic effort and struggle and experiment.

By adding the past, with its volcanic power and creative force, to the present of reason and logical judgment, a superior combination will have been effected. A true whole will have been engendered. Compelled, man will have found the God who abides in the heart of nature. That is a perfection which surely can overcome all problems and difficulties life may present-for the whole person and not simply their parts would be called into active operation. This would truly be evolution, and spiritual development and unfoldment in the finest and highest sense of the term. Metaphysics, if wisely employed, can well become the technique of the future man.

The prayer gesture, therefore, aims to link man by aspiration or by suggestion to the whole vital world of former time when the world was young. That is why prayers and psalms of centuries ago seem to possess so great an efficacy. All harp on the great fundamental truths concerning the power of God in that He created the world, governs it now, and controls all its phenomena. And He can bless His creatures with fruition when they acknowledge Him, as is testified to by so many of the biblical narratives. Thus these prayers tend suggestively to connect the individual today, with events and individuals and divine manifestations of time gone by. If God did so much for Abraham and Solomon and Jesus in those days by virtue of their knowledge of Him, then likewise He can do as much today for me if I follow similar rules as did these men of old. A complex process of auto-suggestion is thus set into operation when the requisite degree of exaltation or concentration–the royal effective roads into the Unconscious–have been achieved. And the contemplation of these blessings and wonders evoke similar conditions from within where God abides.

Robert Anton Wilson

HOW BRAIN SOFTWARE PROGRAMS BRAIN HARDWARE

Robert Anton Wilson

As everybody who uses a computer knows, the software can change the functioning of the hardware in radical and sometimes startling ways. The First Law of Computers–so ancient some claim it dates back to the dark Cthulhoid aeons when LBJ and giant reptiles still roamed the Earth–tells us succinctly, "Garbage In, Garbage Out" (GIGO for short). The wrong software *guarantees* wrong answers. Alternately, the correct software will "solve" previously intractable problems in ways that appear "miraculous" to the majority of domesticated primates at this primitive stage of evolution.

I propose the principle software used in the human brain consists of words, metaphors, disguised metaphors and linguistic structures, in general. I also propose, and will here try to demonstrate, that the Sapir-Whorf- Korzybski Hypothesis, as it is called in sociology– "A change in language can transform our perception of the cosmos"–becomes intuitively obvious with a simple experiment in altering brain software by changing the structure of our language.

The human brain has been called a "three-pound universe" (Judith Hooper), an "enchanted loom" (Charles S. Sherrington), a "bio-computer" (John Lilly), a "hive of anarchy" (Bernard Wolfe), an "intellectual intestine" ("de Selby"), etc., but whatever one calls it, it remains the most powerful data processor known on this planet. The brain, like your desk computer, does not receive raw data. It receives such data as it has been built

Column 1	Column 2
The electron in a wave.	The electron appears as a wave when recorded by an instrument.
The electron is a particle.	The electron appears as a particle when recorded by an instrument.
John is lethargic and unhappy.	John appears lethargic and unhappy in the office.
John is full of fun and high spirits.	John appears full of fun and high spirits while on holiday.
The car involved in the hit-and-run accident was a Ford.	In memory, I think I recall the car involved in the hit-and-run accident as a Ford.
This is a fascist idea	This seems like a fascist idea to me.
Beethoven was better than Mozart.	I enjoy Beethoven more than Mozart.
This is a sexist movie.	This seems like a sexist movie to me.

to receive, and it processes the data according to the programs (software) that have been put into it.

Consider the following columns of easily-comprehensible sentences and see if you can determine the major structural difference between Column 1 and Column 2 considered as software for the human brain.

The first column consists of statements in ordinary English, as heard in common usage at this superstitious and barbaric stage of Terran evolution. These statements all assume the viewpoint which philosophers call "naïve realism"–the belief something called "reality" exists somewhere "out there" beyond our brains, and can be directly perceived by our brains. Scientists, as well as philosophers, now agree that such "realism" can only be described as "naïve," because no two people ever perceive exactly the same "reality" a fact well established in perception psychology, general psychology, sociology, etc. And, in fact, no two animals perceive the same "reality:" each species has its own *umwelt*, or reality-tunnel made up of the signals which the senses and brains of that species can apprehend and comprehend. Worse: instruments perceive different "realities" also, as General Relativity and Quantum Mechanics have amply demonstrated.

It has been emphasized by Niels Bohr, P. W. Bridgman, Bertrand Russell, Count Alfred Korzybski and others that sentences of the sort found in Column 1 not only "ignore" the experimental relativity of perceptions but also subtly condition our brains to "ignore" or forget this relativity, if we ever learned it, or even to avoid noticing it at all. As Korzybski especially emphasized, these "Aristotelian" sentences act as software tending to program us to assume attitudes of dogmatism, unwarranted certitude and intolerance.[1]

By comparison, Column 2 consists of parallel statements rewritten in E-prime, or English-prime, a language based on the work of A. Korzybski and proposed for scientific usage by such authors as D. David Bourland and E. W. Kellogg III. E-prime contains much the same vocabulary as standard English but has been made isomorphic to quantum physics (and modern science generally) by first abolishing the Aristotelian "is" of identity and then reformulating each statement phenomenologically in terms of signals received and interpreted by a body (or instrument) moving in space-time.

Concretely, "The electron is a wave" employs the Aristotelian "is" of identity and thereby introduces the false-to-experience notion we can know the indwelling Aristotelian "essence" or "nature" of the electron. "The electron appears as a wave when recorded with instrument" reformulates the English sentence into E-prime, abolishes the "is" of identity and returns us to an accurate report of what actually transpired in space-time, namely that the electron was constrained by a certain instrument to appear in a certain form of manifestation.

Similarly, "The electron appears as a particle when recorded by instrument," evades Aristotelian dogmatism and forces us to *operationalize* or *phenomenologize* our report by stating what actually happened in space-time, namely that the electron was constrained by a different instrument to appear in a different form of manifestation.

Note well (and please *try* to remember) "The electron is a wave" and "The electron is a particle" create contradiction, and have historically led to debate and sometimes violent quarrel (e.g., "I did not call my learned colleague an jackass. I called him a blithering idiot.") At one time these Aristotelian misstatements (bad software)–attempting to say what an electron "is"–appeared to justify the opinion that parts of physics can only be expressed in terms of almost surrealist paradox– i.e., within the same Aristotelian logical-linguistic structure, many physicists circa 1920 to 1930 were led to proclaim that "The universe is illogical" or "The universe does not make sense," etc.

On the other hand, as Dr. Niels Bohr, the Nobel Prize winning Danish physicist, first noted, the E-prime alternatives–"The electron appears as a wave when constrained by instrument," and "The electron appears as a particle when constrained by instrument" –do not appear *contradictory* but *complementary*. They do not lead to debate or violent quarrel they do not portray the world as bizarre or irrational and (not coincidentally) they simply report what actually took place in the space-time of actual experiments.

Although Bohr did not formulate E-prime-or even Danish-prime, Danish being the language in which he habitually wrote and probably thought-the basis of E-prime can be found in his Principle of Complementarity and the Copenhagen Interpretation of physics which he created in collaboration with his students circa 1926 to 1928.

The American physicist and Nobel laureate P. W. Bridgman first generalized the Bohr approach by articulating the specific principle that scientific propositions should be stated in terms of actual *operations*. If we rigorously follow this rule, we will eventually find ourselves writing E-prime if English serves as our normal language-or in French-prime if we regularly write French, etc. We will have exchanged obsolete Aristotelian software for modern scientific software. We will then program our brains differently, formulate different thoughts and (almost certainly) learn different perceptions or styles of perception.

For the benefit of students of philosophy, although both Bohr and Bridgman appear to have been chiefly influenced by the actual (and startling) experiments in 1920s quantum mechanics, their major intellectual influences appear to have been existentialist philosopher Søren Kierkegaard, in the case of Bohr, and psychologist/philosopher William James, in the case of Bridgman. Thus, the logic of modern physics, and of E-prime, not only serves as an isomorph of the quantum world but also as the natural way to present the key ideas of Existentialism and Pragmatism. As I have already hinted, E-prime also closely resembles the principles of Zen Buddhism and of phenomenological sociology, as influenced by the radical Existentialist Husserl. This suggests that E-prime may not only clarify debates within science but also prove useful in daily life-if we wish to think pragmatically or existentially or in terms of experienced events in space-time rather than thinking metaphysically of "ghosts in the machine;' i.e., abstract essences haunting block-like entities.

Already one suspects a great deal of the misunderstanding of, or total confusion about, certain non-Aristotelian systems derives from the fact that most writers, not habitually using E-prime, have discussed these systems in ordinary English, which introduces Aristotelian structures into non-Aristotelian data and thus breeds chaos and endless paradox. Once again, "Garbage In, Garbage Out:' Aristotelian software does not transduce non-Aristotelian data.

As an experiment, any reader who has had problems understanding quantum physics, Zen, Existentialism or phenomenology should try rereading a book on each and translating all sentences with the Aristotelian "is" to new sentences in E-prime. You may then come to share my suspicion that the difficulties are not found in the subjects but in the use of the wrong language to discuss the subjects–the wrong software for the data.

Looking at the next two sentences in Column 1– "John is lethargic and unhappy" and "John is full of fun and high spirits" –we again encounter contradiction, and we may well suspect pathology. The inexperienced psychiatrist, indeed, might quickly pronounce that John "is" suffering from a manic depressive psychosis. And, of course, others with a less clinical orientation might rush with equal haste to decide that one set of reports must be due to careless observation or downright lies, and accept the opposite reports as totally true. This could lead to lively debate, or actual quarrel about what sort of man John "really is."

(The reader may find it amusing, as I do, that quarrels of this sort–what sort of man John "really is" or what sort of woman Mary "really is"–occur every day in our still-medieval society, even though less than one quarreler in a thousand knows consciously that such debates depend on Aristotelian philosophy and that asking what something "really is" only make sense at all within the context of Aristotelian definitions of "reality" and "is-ness.")

The E-prime translations– "John appears lethargic and unhappy in the office" and "John appears full of fun and high spirits on holiday" –do not contradict each other, report the actual observations in space-time accurately, and remind us that we never know or experience John as an Aristotelian essence (a "spook" in Max Stirner's terms) but only as an aspect of a social field, just as we never know an electron as an Aristotelian essence but only as aspect of an instrumental field.

Another linguistic point seems noteworthy here. I absently wrote "on holiday" because I have spent several years in Ireland; and in Ireland, as in England, people do not go "on vacation," they go "on holiday." The choice of metaphors here does not seem accidental. To say one goes on holiday is to speak the language of the working class, for whom the time off appears merry and playful; but to say one goes on vacation is to speak the language of the ruling class. *Vacation* comes from the same root as vacant and reflects what the owner sees when he looks around the floor–a vacancy where John "should" "be." (I suspect that the owner probably thinks some negative thoughts about the Labor Unions and the "damned Liberal" Government that forced him to pay John even when John "is vacant:') I leave it as a puzzle for the reader: Do the Irish and English speak Working Class in this case because they have had several socialist governments, or have they had several socialist governments because they learned to speak the language of the Working Class? And: has the U.S., alone among industrial nations, never had a socialist government because it speaks the Ruling Class language, or does it speak the Ruling Class language because it has never had a socialist government?

Moving along, "The first man stabbed the second man with a knife," although it contains no explicit Aristotelian "is," continues the Aristotelian assumption that the brain directly apprehends and comprehends "objective" "reality." Dropping this monkish medieval software and trying modern scientific software we get the E-prime translation, "The first man appeared to stab the second man with what appeared to me to be a knife:' This accurately reports the activity of the brain as an instrument in space-time, evades Aristotelian dogmatism, operationalizes or phenomenologizes our software-and, incidentally, may spare us from the traditional embarrassment of psychology students if we happen to land in a class where the instructor inflicts a certain notorious experiment upon us. In the case of that experiment, the first man actually makes stabbing motions, without stabbing or piercing, and with a banana, not a knife. Most students, in most cases where this experiment has been performed, actually see a knife instead of a banana. (Another reason for doubting Aristotelian software: perception and inference mingle so quickly and feed back to each other so totally, that one cannot existentially untangle them.) Together with John-in-the-office and John-on-holiday, this should illustrate vividly that E-prime has applications beyond physics and on into daily life. It should also make clear that the software of Aristotelian structural assumptions in standard English indeed programs the brain to malfunction– "Garbage In, Garbage Out." (Further illustrations of how the brain, running on Aristotelian software, populates the world with hallucinations and projections can be found in my books *Prometheus Rising*, *Quantum Psychology* and *The New Inquisition*, among others.)

Similarly, "The car involved in the hit-and-run accident was a blue Ford" seems inadequate and obsolete Aristotelian-software –as many eye-witnesses have discovered with some pain during skillful cross examination in court. The E-prime translation into modern software, "In memory, I think I recall the car involved in the hit-and-run accident as a blue Ford" would remove a lot of fun from the lives of lawyers but seems more harmonious with what we now know about neurology and perception psychology.

Again, "This is a fascist idea" contains Aristotelian software, unscientifically omits the instrument from the report, and perpetuates dogmatism and intolerance. Translated into post-quantum E-prime software, this becomes "This seems like a fascist idea to me;' which scientifically indicates the instrument being used to constrain the data–in this case, the evaluative apparatus of the speaker's brain. Note one more time that "This is a fascist idea" contradicts "This is not a fascist idea" and provokes quarrels (in which each side seems likely to arrive at the conclusion that the other side "are" damned idiots or worse). "This seems like a fascist idea to me" does not contradict "This doesn't seem like a fascist idea to me" and merely registers the fact that the space-time trajectories of two brains, like two Einsteinian instruments, will yield different readings of the same space-time events.

Our next example, "Beethoven is better than Mozart" might bring the difference between Aristotelian and post-quantum software into clearer focus for many. As formulated in standard English, this assertion implies, if analyzed philosophically, that there exist indwelling essences, or "natures," or spooks, in the music of Beethoven and Mozart, and that Beethoven's spooks "really are" better than Mozart's spooks. Since no such spooks are findable in space-time, the debate about this issue, formulated in this software, can go on forever or until somebody gets so bored that he resorts to blunt instruments to silence the debaters.

The translation into E-prime, "I enjoy Beethoven more than Mozart" reports accurately a series of space-time events–enjoyment processes in the brain of the speaker. This does not contradict another speaker's alternative report, "I enjoy Mozart more than Beethoven," and both reports can profitably be classed as complementary in Bohr's sense.

I cannot resist a minor digression. Although I have only read, and never heard, the endless debate between Mozart maniacs and Beethoven buffs, on one occasion I did hear such a Thomist or medieval debate about composer Bela Bartók. This happened in a restaurant in Dun Laoghaire, Ireland, and the debaters, two *Englishentities* (a word I coined to avoid the human chauvinism implied in *Englishpersons*) grew increasingly heated and hostile as they argued. The male Englishentity insisted that Bartók's music "really is" rubbish and junk and noise, etc. The female English-entity insisted, *au contraire*, that Bartók's music "really is" wonderfully new and experimental and exciting, etc. I found it excruciatingly hard to avoid the temptation to walk over to their table and explain E-prime to them. I think the main reason I resisted the temptation lies in many often-repeated experiences that convinced me that Englishentities recognize an American accent as soon as they hear it and most of them "know," or think they know, that any American– or any other non-Englishentity– ærereally is" stupid and uncultured compared to any Englishentity, and they therefore simply would not have listened to me. Such Englishentities have developed a remarkable skill in looking simultaneously polite and bored while engaged in not listening to non-Englishentities–as the Irish, the Hindus, the Africans and numerous others have noted before me.

Finally, "This is a sexist movie" contains Aristotelian metaphysics implying indwelling essences or spooks within the film. The E-prime translation, "This appears a sexist movie to me" includes the observer and the instrument (the observer's brain) in the report and programs the brain with modern, rather than medieval, software. And, again, "This is a sexist movie" contradicts "This is not a sexist movie," while "This appears a sexist movie to me" does not contradict but complements "This does not appear a sexist movie to me."

(One is tempted to add that the whole *bon ton* debate about sexism "in" movies appears only an "intellectual" sublimation of the older, cruder debate, surviving in more primitive areas, like Little Rock, Arkansas, or the U.S. Congress, about indwelling "obscenity" "in" movies. E-prime software takes the fanaticism out of such debates, removes Aristotelian metaphysics and places us back in the phenomenological world of how individual brains process their experience in space-time.)

A further illustration of these principles appears *apropos*. Once while speaking before the Irish Science Fiction Association at Trinity College, Dublin, I was asked, "Do you believe in UFOs?" Evading the temptation to launch an oration on the disadvantages of the yes-no logic of "belief" and the advantages of the modern logic of probability and percentages, I answered simply, "Yes." The questioner then grew excited and offered a long argument that UFOs "really are" those rare meteorological events called "sundogs." I replied simply that he appeared to believe in UFOs also. He then grew more excited and denied vigorously that he "believed" in UFOs, even though he had just moments earlier argued that 1) UFOs exist and 2) he knew what all of them "really are."

This story amuses me because I have read a great deal of the literature of the UFO debate and almost all of it seems constrained by Aristotelian software processing the brains of the debaters. So-called "Skeptics" can just as accurately be dubbed "Believers:" they merely believe different models than the socalled "Cultists" or heretics. The "Skeptics" believe, very fervently, that "all" UFOs can be identified as "really being" *ordinary* hallucinations, or hoaxes, or sundogs, or heat inversions, or weather balloons, or the planet Venus, etc. The "Cultists" or heretics believe, some as dogmatically as the Skeptics but some (oddly) more tentatively, that "all" –or maybe only some–

UFOs can be identified as spaceships, or time-machines, or secret weapons (of the U.S. or Russia or a hypothetical surviving Nazi underground) or *non-ordinary* hallucinations, etc. Among those who have chosen the model of "non-ordinary" hallucinations, Dr. Carl Gustav Jung proposes that UFOs represent an evolutionarily important eruption of new energies from the "collective unconscious." Dr. Jacques Vallee, a computer scientist, argues that UFOs have been created by brain manipulations of some unscrupulous and unidentified intelligence Agency; and cognitive neuroscientist Dr. Michael Persinger suggests that UFOs result from external-world energy fluctuations–leading to weird lights (probably ball lightning), jumping furniture, electrical malfunctions, etc.–and also altering brain waves so that internal-world hallucinations occur.

From the point of view of Aristotelian software, the important issue appears that of choosing which of these conflicting models to "believe." From the point of view of post-quantum software, the important issue appears that of not "believing" any model but estimating (as far as possible) which model seems most probable in a given case or set of cases. Post-quantum software would also probably incline us to accept Bohr's Principle of Complementarity and accept different models on different occasions, for different space-time events.

It seems probable that the prevalence of Aristotelian software in most brains at this stage of evolution accounts for the ubiquitous prevalence of dogmatic belief in one or another UFO model among both "Skeptics" and "Cultists"–and also explains the relative rarity of multi-model zeteticism.

A more controversial illustration of brain software in action: in Chicago in the 1960s, I knew a pacifist, Joffrey Stewart, who spent most of his waking hours walking the streets distributing anti-war pamphlets. Some of these broadsides

Joffrey had written himself; some had been written by others but seemed worthy of circulation according to Joffrey's standards. However, Joffrey did not distribute anybody's pamphlets without first "correcting" them in accord with his own software or reality-tunnel or system of semantics. Specifically, he would place question marks before and after any word that seemed to him to imply unexamined and nefarious assumptions. The words that bothered Joffrey most seem to have been "our" and "we." If you received a leaflet by, say Noam Chomsky or Dave Dellinger, after it had been revised by Joffrey, you would see sentences like the following (I am paraphrasing from memory, but I believe I capture the spirit of Joffrey's Criticism of Language):

"...and? our? taxes are being used to napalm infants..."
"...to defend? our? standard of living..."
"...these atrocities? we? are committing..." "...and why, after all, are? we? in Vietnam?"

It appears the Aristotelian "is" of identity should not be considered the only glitch in our brain software. Joffrey Stewart's question marks certainly led me to revise my own software. When I heard Mr. Reagan described as "our President," I think of Joffrey writing this as "?our? President," and, then, of course, I recall less than twenty-five percent of eligible voters elected Mr. Reagan, the other seventy-five-plus percent either voted for somebody else or showed their skepticism and/or contempt by not voting at all.

At this point it seems advisable to quote Korzybski; "I have said what I have said; I have not said what I have not said." For instance, a while back I set a little trap for careless and ideologically-impassioned readers, by pointing out that in a specific context the word "sexism" should only be used in relation to evaluative processes in the brain of the speaker. From this existentialist-phenomenologist (or operationalist) truism, certain readers probably deduced the inaccurate conclusion, "This author denies that anything to be called sexism exists in the objective world at all." Once again, the wrong software caused the signals to go awry.

Nothing in my remarks implied that using the word "sexism" to describe a company that pays female workers wages averaging less than fifty percent of comparable male workers' wages should be related only to the evaluative activities of the brain of the commentator. Quite the contrary. The operationalist approach here would relate the word "sexism" to the economic data demonstrating the measurable existence of the wage differential.

An old example in physics will clarify this. If an iron bar has a measured temperature of ninety-eight degrees Fahrenheit, what would you expect to find in measuring the temperature of an electron in the bar?

If you guess ninety-eight degrees Fahrenheit, you appear to be using the wrong software. If you say that the question cannot be answered without more data, I suspect you still haven't got the right software for this test.

Some books will tell you that "an electron has no temperature:' More accurately, I think, one should say that the word "temperature" has scientific meaning at, or above, the molecular level, but has no meaning below the molecular level. Temperature measures the *movement* of molecules and hence cannot be meaningfully applied to sub-molecular processes.

Thus, to say "sexism" must be considered operationally to refer to evaluations in a brain when speaking of art works does not mean that "sexism" must always refer only to such internal matters. When speaking of economic practices, "sexism" has meaning in relation to economic statistics. This parallels the situation in physics, where "temperature" refers to molecular movement in meaningful statements, and loses all meaning when one attempts to apply it to sub-molecular phenomena.

In conclusion, I would like to suggest, again, that these arguments for post-quantum software (language structures) have as much application and practicality outside science as within science. The cutting edge of philosophy-everything that can be called post-Nietzschean–represents a similar struggle against the increasingly obvious malfunctions of Aristotelian categories; one finds this recognized among such seemingly opposed groups as the Cambridge Linguistic Analysts and the Paris Situationists. Modern literature at its liveliest or most inventive–I think of Joyce, Pound, Borges, Faulkner, Beckett, O'Brien, Williams, Burroughs, Ginsberg–represents a series of strategies to break out of the Aristotelian software of our culture by creating non-Aristotelian linguistic grids. Modern painting took on non-Aristotelian traits as early as 1907 and music at about the same time. To the extent that we remain hypnotically entranced by Aristotelian language structures we become isolated not only from science–and, as I have hinted, from such exotic and interesting systems as Buddhism–but also from the lively and innovative part of modern culture generally.

Sculpture by Jeff Mandon

The Rebel In Us All
Jeff Mandon

When I was first asked to write a chapter for inclusion in this book, I considered the title and balked a little; after all it's a very provocative title. I didn't want to find myself in a position of identifying with Satanism and worshiping Lucifer; not because I think it's wrong or immoral but I believe the choosing of it is self-limiting; a losers' game ultimately, for reasons I'll get into a little later. So, what was Lucifer's rebellion? The Bible tells the story of Lucifer being the most beautiful angel in heaven who falls after his attempt to usurp God. That was supposedly the first rebellion. Obviously, it's a metaphor, but I think a somewhat accurate one. It's at least a place to start.

A few years back, I was in a position where, after years of study and practice, my kundalini began to rise. For those unfamiliar with the kundalini; in short, the kundalini is a metaphysical energy system that is located at the base of the spine; as it unfolds and rises up the spine, the person is altered in both their perception, and their higher sensory abilities. The kundalini is said to be the vessel of the Holy Spirit, and I can attest to that, for I found myself falling in love with the Holy Spirit of a lover I had been seeing.

I frame it that way because the Holy Spirit is not some one-size-fits-all spirit or ghost, but as we are individuated, so is the Holy Spirit individuated for us, that he may be our absolute perfect lover complement in every way that is conceivably possible given the circumstance of being disincarnate. My heart was invested by the Holy Spirit for about nine months, and those nine months were like spiritual Boot Camp. I was placed in serious training, guided by my beloved's Holy Spirit himself. And I learned a lot. All the questions I had labored with about our origins, and the Holy Spirit, and Christ consciousness, were answered. Also, I was able to perform with an unusually high ability in terms of telepathy, clairsentience, clairaudience, clairvoyance, and energetic healing.

The point of rebellion is to relieve oneself of the constraints of society; cast off those shackles of convention that we might gain authenticity. To rebel simply for the sake of rebelling is ridiculous, for it is remarkably juvenile in its approach to life. I know because I did it for years in my youth. I mean, after all, every teenager thinks he's Holden Caulfield from *Catcher in the Rye*, or James Dean. Far too many of us are rebels in search of a cause.

Now I do want to a point out that it enables you to find yourself, which is a wonderful thing. But to continue to search for yourself after you have found yourself, simply because you don't feel like working on yourself is, quite frankly, the direct road to emotional infantilization; and there is already far too much of that in the world. So just as a small checkpoint, once you find yourself, the rest of your life will be about working to dismantle some of the unworkable habits and inauthentic aspects of self that were likely created out of a need to protect oneself at the time of their childhood creation. But no matter how you got them by the time you hit twenty or twenty-five, they're yours now.

Hope you will excuse the above digression. So, let's get back to the original rebellion of Lucifer. As I discuss in a soon to be published memoir of sorts called, *Crumbs and Other Things I've Followed Home*, what was shared with me by spirit was a version of the beginning that makes sense to me, and in fact explains a lot. And just for clarity, I'm not saying I was so special to have this amazing experience happen; this investment by the Holy Spirit and all that came with it. When I asked spirit why I was getting this information; I mean after all, why me? Who was I? What I heard very clearly was, "You simply asked the right questions." And I believe that to be true. So first we ask how, if God is all, Lucifer even existed as an opposition to Him? So let's take a look at the premise of God. God is All, meaning He is totally omnipotent, omniscient, and omnipresent. So how can something that is omnipresent have an opposite? Wouldn't it by definition be impossible to be other than that? Other than God? And if God is perfect love, then how could something other than that emanate from him? And we know that something other than perfect love did manifest because to put it to you straight, we're living in it. A realm of imperfection predicated on separation; which is not exactly a walk in the park, generally speaking.

If you believe all that most people of spirit, spirituality and religion profess to believe of God, how can we account for our presence here? For here's the rub; the paradox; how does God exist as omnipotent and of perfect love and that's all, meaning nothing but love, without degree or separation? I mean something's got to give. It's either us or Him. One of us is not real and most people believe their five senses and make the conscious or unconscious decision at this point that it's God who is not really real, not really here, and we who are the genuine article. Let's continue to look at God and what we profess he is. Firstly, how can he create without some form of separation? There has to be a place where something did not exist and now it does. There has to be a point in reality in which the table stops and the sculpture on it begins. Inherent separation on which this realm is predicated. So the first thing we are asked to accept is that God is able to create without any degree of separation; something totally unknown to us. But if God created us and we are creative, then God Himself must be creative too. He just does it in a way that we don't understand, and we can't understand; because if we fully did, the notion of absolute perfection would be brought into this divided realm, and it would cease to be absolute perfection.

Next up, if God is only perfect love, then how do we explain this realm we live in; because it is clearly not of perfect love; and to try to cover it with some hackneyed version of, "Well everything that happens and exists in this world is God's will. God's creation or it wouldn't be here." It is an insult to God and any thinking man's intelligence. If it is all a reflection of the will of a God of perfect love, I think He could come up with something a little bit better than babies in dumpsters. But let's not avoid the real fundamental question here and the answer is a paradox and we're living in it. God could exist as we described him: omnipresent, omnipotent absolutely perfect love; or we can exist as we know us to be. But both can't exist together. Both can't be true. Something's got to give. And that is where most people give up on God and trust instead in only their five senses.

I believe that is a fundamental mistake most of us make. Now I'm not suggesting that we are not here on some level, but the level we are here on is not an eternal one therefore not in fact Real in the absolute sense. Everything of the physical realm is temporal which is as it should be, because if everything here were truly eternal and perfect, and truly Real; the whole thing would be torn apart in a second, for it is all based on separation; and if separation were to become an absolute, all existence would be destroyed in an instant. And in fact, given that time in a line is an illusion of the mind, the physical realm would never have come into being to begin with.

I believe in God because I've had first-hand knowledge and experience of him, so it makes it pretty hard to deny His reality. His presence, however, is another matter. The long and short of it is that His presence here depends directly on us. God will not go against our free will. And we have free will because free will is necessary for one to create, and we are creative because God is creative and we are chips off the old block. His sons.

And God is perfect love. He exists here to the degree that we bring love through. And I mean as much as He or Love is held in our thoughts, our words, and through our actions; and subsequently our character and our lives themselves which are affected, and enriched as a result. So, the game is a simple one, and a somewhat self-serving one; to the degree that we love and choose love, God will exist in this realm. The reason is because God is love. He is in every drop of loving existence. And because of that, I tell you no act of love, however small, is ever wasted. But know this, there is no such thing as a neutral thought or a neutral action. It is always in our power to choose either fear or love; and that choice has definite ramifications on both ourselves and the state of the world we live in. The long and short of things is, since God is perfect love, and since Lucifer or ego or evil or the devil or whatever you want to call him seduced the Yin quality in God the father just prior to the point where time and the Big Bang began, to stop making eternal love to its Yang counterpart, just long enough to step back and observe her beloved.

Sounds so easy, so innocent. But to have knowledge of something there must be separation. There must be observer and observed. And as physics now tells us there is no such thing as an impartial observer. Our presence influences the activity on a subatomic level. So the notion that we're to sit on a fence somewhere and not hurt anybody, needs to be laid to rest, as it is not possible. We are all active participants in this game. It's impossible for us not to be. So let's start showing up more fully and better equipped for the game.

So the Bible tells us that Eve ate of the tree of knowledge which is symbolic of the moment where separation became a thought contemplated or considered by some aspect of God. It is inevitable because if God is All, every conceivable thought, including the thought of annihilation disguised as simple separation, instituted by a very dark entity whose evil we should not underestimate, must rise in turn for consideration. And it probably sounded so great. "Just step back a moment to admire your beloved." And that's all it took, because knowledge, as in the tree of knowledge, is predicated on observer and observed. In other words, it is predicated on some form of separation. And that seemingly innocent act, could have been the end of it All if God were not God every bit as great as we believe him to be.

Since God could not be less than himself, he could not be destroyed by separation, for his omnipresence did not allow separation to manifest inside Him; inside His realm of existence of absolutes, true eternity, and genuine perfection, because to do so would have destroyed everything in all creation. Everything that ever was, is, or could be would burst into nothingness when separation became an absolute. God's nature had a remedy for this, which was to provide a little bubble of sorts where the manifestation of separation could exist since all thoughts of God without exception manifest on some level. This level which houses us, is the lowest and densest one. And we call it the universe with the physical realm. But the metaphysical realm burst into creation at the same time we did. The moment the concept of separation and aloneness apart from the

All was entertained by God. He burst into absolute existence with a resounding "I am" for the concept of separation forced the thought of, "Am I?" On God and the instantaneous response was, as I said, "I AM!" In that moment of consideration brought about let's say by Lucifer's rebellion as it were, all of creation, in terms of the physical universe, blew into existence in a moment the scientists called the Big Bang. And since it was his thought, predicated on all that God is not, Lucifer now stood as top dog on home turf.

But God in his mercy did not allow us to fall into this realm alone, for that would've meant our complete and utter destruction, if love were absent from the equation. So God created a bubble of sorts to hold this paradox. And we exist in it, as does heaven itself, given that even in heaven there is evidence of individuation of souls, angels, etc. and any degree of individuation is predicated on some amount of separation therefore the metaphysical realm must indeed be part of the paradox bubble we inhabit. But there is more to life than this. There is a point of refinement where separation ceases to exist, and the infinite and absolutes return, and perfect love reigns. This is the realm of God the father.

There's a reason why our world contains no absolutes; we can approximate them but we can't actualize them to the point of perfection and I mean true perfection, or true infinity, or any genuine absolute. It's because this realm was meant to be temporary. The holding cell if you like until we can get back to a genuine reunion with God the eternal absolute, and a healing of the rift between heaven and earth. This is not only possible but is achievable without outside assistance. By that I mean nothing is going to swoop down out of the sky and rescue us, and bring us home. This was designed to be, and has to be therefore, an inside job. We have to pull it off ourselves working with just what we have at our disposal. Ourselves, meaning both physical and metaphysical aspects, and love which is the presence of the divine. And the kundalini rising in answer to God's call, which is itself a bit of the pixie dust necessary for us to fly.

But it is not the whole of the issue. The real core is love. The real determining factor is based on how much love we can pull through into this realm, and it will be done primarily, at the start, by two people falling in love and making love who happen to be twin flames. This will be the point of origin for the healing of this realm and its reunion with heaven and God the father.

For when the Big Bang occurred and we split off into this illusion; and I deem it an illusion purely because it is not eternal and knows no absolutes, and as quantum physics will tell us, is contrived largely of our own projections. This gift God's very being gave us, rather than deliver us to the horror of true separation from the All, which is what Lucifer was going for. He wanted to create a little realm where he could replace God as king. Where he could at last usurp God and replace him as head man... But God decided to put us to sleep with our illusion of separation instead of leaving us to that fate for all eternity. And God has continued to watch over us trying in vain to encourage us to choose love if for no other reason than self-interest, and I trust, weeping with us as the dream we fell into has slowly turned into a nightmare. And he went one step further. He did something that only a perfect loving God would do. He came with us into this dream to the degree he could, in keeping with the circumstances. For in that moment of the Big Bang where an almost infinite number of souls or spirits were created; because remember there are no absolutes in this realm; so in fact an actual finite number of souls were created; and God invested Himself in the Sacred Heart of every single soul or being that individuated. He could not stop us from experiencing the separation, for on some level we chose it when we allowed ourselves to be seduced by Lucifer to rebel by considering the notion of separation from the All, but God put the brakes on the ultimate annihilation that would've occurred by lending his presence in the form of infusing this creation with natural love.

But how is it possible for us to individuate without destroying God? Or at least invalidating his quality of being one and All without degree or separation? Imagine a prism through which a beam of white light is passed, that beam of light will project on the other side as a rainbow of colors. And that rainbow contains every, well just shy of every (not quite infinite) color in existence. So every color in existence to the degree possible in this realm, can be created without actually altering the white light itself, at all. It's almost an optical illusion. Now, every color of that almost infinite myriad of colors represents an individual soul. So, say we have a soul whose various aspects altogether create as its signature presents, a particular shade of red, and that is its color; singular and impossible to duplicate. On the color wheel its opposite will have a distinct, singular, exact green color which represents the individual who is their perfect loving complement. What some call their twin flame. Where a soulmate is a general match, the twin flame is the exact beloved God has created for this individual. The speck of God that is in their Sacred Heart which many call the Christ consciousness or the Cosmic consciousness is of a nature that makes it the absolute complement of its counterpart; and here's the wild part: when these two complementary colors are brought together, they merge; and together comprise white light again. In the same way with numbers, that one individual might aspect in a way that generates the percentage 35%. Its twin flame will be an identity that boils down to the moniker 65%. Together they create 100%. But so too could another complementary color or individual that generates the percentage 22% when met with their twin flame would merge with their counterpart who equals 78 % to again create a total of 100%. Your Holy Spirit is not just some one-size-fits-all spirit or ghost. It is literally an echo of your twin flame's Christ consciousness.

For instance, to use our previous example, if my twin flame's color is some hue of red, his Holy Spirit will individuate as the exact hue of green that is the perfect complement to his red. Now ironically, that perfect red, will be the exact red found in my Sacred Heart. It is literally my Christ consciousness echoing as his Holy Spirit to find him and guide him to me. By the same token, my Holy Spirit individuated perfectly for me will be that exact hue of green that exists in his Sacred Heart as his Christ consciousness. So when I invite the Holy Spirit into my heart, it is an act of completion or at least the seeking of completion; for the Holy Spirit and Christ consciousness merge and become whole, with the Holy Spirit representing the Yin aspect and the Christ consciousness acting as the Yang aspect of the whole that is God. Pure white light. 100%.

But they serve two different functions. They are both aspects of the divine. One is inside you from the start which is the Christ consciousness through which you process God's will and how to enact it. It is the doing aspect. The Holy Spirit must be invited into your soul in a moment of sanity which you are definitely having if you are sane enough to invite him in. And because what happens after that may be a return to delusion, once invited in, the Holy Spirit will never leave. He will stay with you through thick and thin. And it is his job to advise you on solving your problems. No matter how big or small, as a problem arises, its perfect answer arises in Him in perfect tandem; for the Holy Spirit is our conduit back to God the father.

So he knows all there is to know about the earthly situation and yet he still has his other foot in the divine of God the father. And the answer He provides is always an appropriate face of love. Though bear in mind sometimes that face of love is self-love and self-protection, which means sometimes the loving response to someone is, "No."

So should two twin flames meet and fall in love and be spiritually developed enough that their kundalini might rise in tandem; their coming together, if you'll excuse the pun, can kick off the return to God. And sex in terms of gender or sexual identity of the participants is irrelevant. Because if you're gay, your twin flame will be gay as well. If you're a man and you're straight, your perfect complement will be a woman. Therefore, everyone has an equal opportunity to be the ultimate hero in this mass awakening. The initial result of this merger of these two twin flames, will be that their kundalini will rise enough that they can hear each other in their sacred hearts due to the presence of the echo of the other one's Christ consciousness in the form of the Holy Spirit which will be invested in the heart of their twin flame, and vice versa. So they should be able to be in separate rooms and yet accurately reflect what the other one is experiencing, saying, and doing; for they will literally have a piece of one another in their sacred hearts. And the messages that they will be giving will be of such Real love that it will be inimitable. For obvious reasons, this will be impossible to fake, which is good news, for it will give us all faith and hope. Hope that God did not forget us. Hope that we are not being punished for our initial rebellion with Lucifer. And we will find that God never judged us to begin with, knowing that it was an unforeseeable circumstance.

It is only God's being that saved us from total destruction. That's the irony of it all. Had Lucifer succeeded in creating this little kingdom after really usurping God, all existence would have been torn apart by the injection of separation without love to soften the blow. So everything, including Lucifer, would've been blown out of existence.

While the Holy Spirit can guide you to your beloved, it involves each of us treating each other with higher regard than we have been. With greater care and love that we might inadvertently lead one another closer and closer with each contact; with each interaction, closer to coming together with our truly beloved. That is what I saw when I asked God how we get home. We have become so warped, that two twin flames actually meeting each other and falling in love without rejection by their own egos or society mores, is getting harder and harder, and rarer and rarer. But we have to hold our faith in God; and more to the point, in one another. Because every rebel really wants to come home in the end. But to return home changed; to get home as their authentic selves.

That is only possible if we are open to choosing love. Loving thought, word, action; and to do so, particularly when we would normally choose to act on some aspect of fear. For we always insert a little separation between us and our proposed object of derision before we judge them; before we deny them. And it is incredibly unhealthy and it really needs to stop. We are truly and irrevocably all in this together. Because from this initial meeting of the twin flames; if it is successful, their abilities will inspire others who will answer God's call by allowing their kundalini to rise in answer to Him. And more and more people will be led to their twin flame. And more and more people will begin to contribute loving thought, word, and deed to this merger of heaven and earth; until, in keeping with the hundredth monkey scenario, there will be a tipping point; a preponderance of participants acting in love, that will flip the world to where everyone awakens at last, and heaven will join with us, and the rift will be healed forever, and the nightmare of a dream pass away. For it was never really separation that Lucifer wanted. That was an unexpected by-product of his desire to replace God. And think for a second, as existentially terrified as we are on a subconscious level at being torn from the bosom of God, and separated forever from the All; Lucifer is even more terrified, for he not only represents fear and is comprised of fear; but experiences fear in its raw, almost ultimate, form. And it is so intense, it blinds him to God's being, to his presence; for when he looks around this world, this turf of his, he thinks he's won. That he has killed God, because as the only entity without a soul, he is unable to see God or experience love. So he has that terror to contend with; For I believe that he is comprised of our collective fearful thoughts. He is in fact, like a big scary Charlie McCarthy doll, where we all contribute to animating him to where he seems to have a mind and life of his own; a consciousness. Much like AI. He is an imitation of life but his lack of a soul renders him blind and deaf to Love's call. Blind and deaf to God himself, who is all manner of love and only love. So without a soul to know love and God with, he thinks he's won; that he has, in fact, conquered God; for there is nothing in evidence to the contrary for him. We know better because we have the Sacred Heart in which the Christ resides and if we are lucky, the Holy Spirit too, conjoined with our Christ.

May be as the final act of housecleaning when heaven and earth are reunited, God will grant Lucifer; Ego; a soul. Maybe He will invest this collection of his children's errant creative energies; the only thing created by His sons not He the father, with an eternal piece of Himself. And perhaps, since He is not only Almighty but all merciful, He will grant this new soul, a twin flame of its own. Only God knows. But I wouldn't be at all surprised. *Go Love!*

Martial Arts: Path of Unification
Daniel Pineda

THE MIRROR OF TRUTH

*"From the beginning, [all that is] discrete
must have its unification,
the divided must be combined."*
—Marshal Yeuh Pei
from *Ten Important Theses*

Man is by nature a maker and user of tools. The first and most potent tool he must learn to use is his own organism. During early socialization he is taught to divide himself into "mind" and "body," and to view the world around him as divided realms of "inner" and "outer:' Though this partition begins as a convenience of speech, it eventually becomes his accepted state of being. The resulting atrophy has become so common among us that most never even consider anything is wrong.

Each personality innovates its own ways to seek pleasure or avoid pain. The materialist runs hard and fast from the smoke-like objects of thought, emotion, and imagination toward the tangible or "real world." Conversely, the intellectual retreats from physicality, seeking the seemingly consequence free mental activities of philosophy, academia, and spirituality. The repressed tendencies and natural appetites morph into the illnesses of obsession, fear, or some other non-equilibrium.

Throughout history, oppressors have kept slaves ignorant of the written word to maintain their control. In this same way the limitations of the mind control the body. Likewise, the mind may be limited by the body, as when a person is hungry, sick, or under constant threat of attack. Tyrants have exploited the unity of man, attacking the particular in him so as to infect the universal. They continually seek to separate him from the treasures of his estate to maintain the illusions of division and polarity.

But the fact remains; man is one being. He cannot be divided without consequence. Yet the problem lies not in what a man is, but in what he understands himself to be. The person who fully understands him or herself to be a unified current can begin to act consciously as a force of nature. Such a person can scale new heights of human achievement–though this cannot occur without the destruction of tyranny.

The unification of man can only occur when he realizes his understanding of himself is incomplete. He must meet and name the fractured pieces of his existence if he endeavors to harmonize and unite them.

Think of the world in which we live. Is it not at times dangerous? Can we ever expect graciousness, love, or selflessness from the inhabitants of such a world? In whom can we place our trust when the earth shakes, famine strikes, disease runs rampant and those we elect or otherwise rely on to maintain the contract of governance fail us time and again? By what method, if any, can a person immediately begin the work of honest self-discovery to bridge the gap between the fractured and unified man? Can you as an individual afford not to learn the answer to these questions?

ENTER THE MARTIAL ARTS

> *"**Budo** is a divine path established by the gods that leads to truth, goodness, and beauty; it is a spiritual path reflecting the unlimited, absolute nature of the universe and the grand design of creation."*
>
> – Morihei Ueshiba
> from *Budo*

The art of fighting is difficult. It is difficult to teach, learn, or even discuss without missing its essence. There are innumerable styles of training that aim to develop attributes in the student the founder thought would aid them in an attack. The root of all these styles is the same because the goal is the same. The goal is to have *Gung Fu*, or "skill acquired through hard work."

The martial arts, or *Budo* as they are called in Japan and *Gung Fu* or *Quan Fa* in China, are the accumulated body of knowledge that includes and synthesizes the numerous ways of defeating an enemy in combat. Generally speaking, this includes all manners of weaponry, technology, and psychological and hand-to-hand warfare, known as martial science. For our current purpose we here refer mainly to unarmed or close-quarters combat methods. In addition to the fighting applications, these methods promote harmony in the self, family, nation, and the world. All of these aspects are collectively known as the martial way.

Martial artists devote themselves to the highest standard of conduct and self-cultivation. They aim to elevate the sciences they study to the level of art. Such a person makes combat with his own ignorance and ultimately seeks harmony. Anyone, regardless of social status, physical limitations, occupation, or religion can choose to become a martial artist simply by dedicating himself to the training and ideals of the martial way.

The need for effective methods of personal defense should be apparent to even the most casual student of history and human nature. In the first book of the bible we find murder, deception, natural disaster, and exile. Even in a biblical world with an ever-watchful creator, the patriarchs encounter danger and trouble constantly. However, through martial prowess they defeated their enemies and established a nation. This is also true of all the ancient tales of gods and men, such as in the Sanskrit epic *The Ramayana* or Homer's *Iliad*, where great heroes kept the light of the world bright and clear through the toils of war.

The way people have successfully deposed the darkness of tyranny and brought an end to injustice is neither random nor haphazard. There is a science to the moral, physical, and spiritual training of free men and women who can defend their liberties against all comers. The way of victory must be learned, practiced, and perfected in order to yield success.

It is almost certain that in at least one instance in life an individual or group will be the target of a person or persons seeking to harm them in some way. If this attack escalates to a physical confrontation, the defender must use a fighting technique to neutralize the attacker(s). The difference between the purely physical and utilitarian martial sciences and the holistic martial arts is that the former is only concerned with how to kill the enemy. The latter is concerned both with a physical and a moral victory. This victory must come about with an appropriate, non-excessive amount of force–and if possible, it makes an attack less likely to occur in the first place.

Because all violence happens within a certain context, it is impossible to divorce these two aspects from one another without creating either A) a sociopathic killer who responds with lethal force at the slightest chance of conflict or B) a lofty thinking, albeit impotent and delusional role player who couldn't stop any assailant. The true martial artist seeks to stop the evil not only in his enemy but also in himself.

What makes this path different from many others is that here the philosophical flows from the practical. The techniques of the martial arts are analogous to verses from the Holy Scriptures. The techniques and strategies of the martial arts are the union of the ideal and the actual, or of science and religion. They are the word made flesh, and unlike other systems of personal development or artistic expression, there can be no purely subjective interpretations. The combative methods are either effective or they are not. Yet you cannot read them; you must DO them in order to gain their import.

Although the same is true of any spiritual instruction, many times this truth gets lost in the endless metaphysics, dogma, and mystery that partition the theory of a system from its practice. It is by doing these techniques that unite the once divided man and transform his organism into an instrument of his Will. The student must achieve coordination because in essence, freedom is the result of coordination.

Martial arts techniques are the alphabet of fighting. Just as we string together letters to make words, so the techniques of combat connect in order to form patterns of strategic and tactical approaches. Every martial art has its own set of basic techniques and patterns that constitute the particular hypothesis of its method.

In the repetitive practice of these movements the many parts of a person begin to unify with greater and greater coordination. At first the neophyte must consciously Will his mind to relax and his body to either flow or crash, depending on the situation. Then, without notice and if almost by accident, he moves in the correct way without thought or reflection; his mind and body become one transparent lens through which the unfettered Will shines clearly and instantaneously. When the student initially notices this phenomenon it shocks him back into his formerly fractured state. But as the frequency of the occurrence increases, so does his comfort and trust in the unknown within himself. The movements he performs eventually seem less his act and become more his being. Over time he learns that whom he calls "I" is in constant motion and inseparable from the rest of his universe of perception. The body is a microcosm. By working on the creation, preservation, and destruction of the body through martial arts, the student engages in initiation through the most potent symbol in the arsenal of self-discovery.

> *"You should become mature in your discipline of Chi, and master the mind."*
> *"It is easy to know the mysterious function of the mind, but difficult to penetrate deep within yourself and act with complete freedom."*
> – Issai Chozanshi
> from *The Demon's Sermon on the Martial Arts*

You won't get very far in the martial arts before you run into its most controversial, least understood, and most misrepresented concept: *Chi* (Chinese) or *Ki* (Japanese). A lot of ideas are associated with Chi, which literally translates as "breath," but is also used to describe the "life force" or "vital energy" flowing through all things. All martial arts utilize Chi with varying levels of emphasis, and all have differing theories on how it may be put to use.

The systems that stress the development of Chi, and insist that proper technique flows from its cultivation, are generally known as soft or internal martial arts. These include styles like Tai Chi Chuan, Baguazhang, Hsing Yi Chuan, and Aikido. The arts that focus on body conditioning through the direct application of muscular development and skeletal toughening are known as hard or external martial arts. These include the styles of Shaolin Chuan Fa, Shotokan Karate, and Muay Thai. Most arts are a combination of both internal and external, such as Liu He Ba Fa, Jujutsu, Taijutsu, and Escrima. A common saying in the martial arts is "from hard to soft and from soft to hard."

There have been many outrageous claims made about Chi. These include that Chi can stop bullets, levitate you at Will, or allow you to knock out opponents without touching them. Understandably, this has given the more practical exponents of the martial way a negative view on the entire subject. Yet amazing things do tend to happen when a high level of Chi cultivation has been achieved. Some of the more accepted results of Chi training are accelerated healing, longevity, mental control, and relaxation, all of which enhance one's life and martial arts practice.

At the foundation of the theory of Chi is that our intentions can lead the life force and should therefore be disciplined toward harmony. This is perhaps the most important aspect of Chi training–that illness is the result of imbalance. First achieving balance within themselves, martial artists then seek to make the world around them better.

Here are some basic exercises to build your endurance, focus, coordination, and therefore, your Chi:

Chi Exercise 1: Baby Breathing

When most adults breathe they do so with only the upper part of the chest, and with a great deal of tension in the torso. This is not very conducive to relaxation, mental balance, or Chi cultivation. In contrast, babies breathe from the lower abdomen using their entire bodies in a relaxed manner. The Ancients reasoned that in order to achieve suppleness and natural power we should mimic the newborn child's breathing.

To practice Baby Breathing, lie down and place one hand on your chest and the other on your belly just bellow the navel. This is called the "Lower Dan Tien," and is your physical center of gravity as well as the place where you store the most Chi (the lower abdomen is called the "sea of Chi").

Next, breathe deeply and rhythmically, moving the hand on your belly up and down without moving the hand on your chest.

When you master this technique while lying down you can then begin training it while sitting, standing, and walking.

Only when you breathe this way without conscious effort will you reap the benefits of Baby Breathing. Learning to breathe this way is vital to your growth as a martial artist.

Chi Exercise 2: Wuji Standing Posture

Wuji means "no extreme;' and according to Taoist sages it is the source of the cosmos. By standing in the Wuji Posture, the source-posture for all others, you cultivate balance and greater awareness.

To practice the Wuji Posture, stand naturally with your feet a few inches apart and hands down at your sides. Slightly bend the knees, tuck the pelvis in and hollow out the chest. Lightly touch your tongue to the roof of the mouth.

Chi Exercise 3: Cheng Bao Posture

Cheng Bao means "embracing:' This posture is important for acquiring martial power and learning how the various parts of the body are interconnected.

To practice the Cheng Bao Posture, first stand in Wuji Posture and spread your feet hip to shoulder width apart. Then raise the hands with your palms facing down and arms slightly bent until they reach shoulder height. Finally, turn your palms inward to stand as if you are embracing a tree or pillar.

WHEN THE PUPIL IS READY ...

"Self-will is the only virtue that takes no account of man-made laws. A self-willed man obeys a different law, the one law I hold absolutely sacred–the law in himself, his own "will."

– Bruce Lee
Founder of *Jeet Kune Do*

We live in an era when the masters of the various styles and countries may be observed with relative ease via books, videos, and the Internet. In the past this was not the case; it was a very rare privilege to be exposed to such a wide array of teachings. By watching these masters we see the similarities in each method's application. In almost every case martial arts experts display the attributes of balance, power, focus, sensitivity, and coordination. Find an instructor who embodies these attributes. The feats of these men and women draw us to the source of their power, like concentric rings that betray where the pebble struck the pond.

The training that enables the correct cultivation and use of power has its foundation in discipline. Discipline is the first step. If you are to make combat with an enemy, either internal or external, your tools must move on command and without hesitation. The mind must obey, the body must obey, and they must be taught to work together before they unite and can be trusted to tend to themselves. This requires long years of training.

This means that whatever training or art you decide to study, you must give yourself entirely to the work. Show up to class and practice what you are taught. Keep yourself in the best physical and mental shape possible, refraining from anything that would inhibit your growth as a martial artist. Resign yourself to the fact that the journey of the martial arts ends when you die, and not a moment sooner.

When the student initially comes to the master he expects to be taught. But before the master can transmit the science of victory he must first train the pupil to receive pain without emotional distress. This is because the martial arts cannot be described; they must be *felt* in order to perceive exactly how they work.

A master martial artist can demonstrate his power. This demonstration may not be what the student expects, but it will be present nonetheless because it is the master's duty to find a student he can entrust his knowledge to. The true master prefers to show rather than tell, and whenever possible will demystify rather then conceal his methods. Although he is not perfect, if the master honestly conveys the method he knows to be effective he can lead the student to a vision of perfection. As long as the vessel holds pure water drink from it and don't worry about its shape or material.

It is ultimately the pupil's mistake to think the knowledge he is gaining is what will make him great. The master could forget everything he knows and still be the master because he has transmuted his essence. If he ceases to speak, it does not the change the source of his speech. If he ceases to be, it does not change the source of his being. The student should place himself firmly on the path of comprehending the source of the master's teachings, and endeavor to change himself at the deepest level in order to be one with that source.

Above all, keep going.

Glyphs from the Mayan Calendar

Apocalypse Never? A Refutation of the Eschaton
Robert Brazil

Listen up pilgrims: the world will not end in 2012 AD We are not going to be judged by a flaming sword-toting, gargantuan, atmospheric Christ. The dead are not going to rise from their graves to be reanimated for glory or eternal hellfire. Quetzalcoatl is not returning to obliterate humanity, nor will legions of saucers piloted by beneficent Astral Brothers arrive in the nick of time to whisk away true believers.

As we approach the millennium of the western Gregorian calendar, people worldwide are going nuts with anticipation. Remarkably, millions of people yearn for an Armageddon, for a final judgment of humanity, for the end of time and history. In the past we witnessed the remarkable messianic martyrdom of David Koresh's Branch Davidians; the incomprehensible mass murder/suicide of Luc Jouret's bogus Rosicrucian Solar Temple; and the over-the-top shenanigans of Japan's Aum Shinrikyo cult, which, growing tired of waiting for the apocalypse, decided to hasten it through high-tech mass murder.

However guilty the FBI and ATF are for the Waco Massacre, they fulfilled Koresh's own prophecy, at least symbolically. And this is a crucial point. To David Koresh, the ATF represented the forces of Satan and Leviathan. In his complete scenario, the Davidians' martyrdom would be followed by their immediate resurrection, to witness Koresh stand with Jesus in the Judgment and punishment of the world. That part didn't happen, and it's not too hard to figure out why-every prophecy of the total destruction of mankind by God has failed.

These are just a few of the most extreme and visible examples. And nobody had even heard of these groups before they came roaring to celebrity with guns, gasoline, and nerve-toxins. Equally dangerous, but far more subtle, are ultra-fundamentalist Christian groups that see the Second Coming and Armageddon as the only solution to humanity's discords and lusts. It is reasonable to fear that an apocalyptic Christian U.S. president could "push the button" to speed things up on World War III, just to hasten the "rapture." In the 1980s, Ronald Reagan, a true believer, had the motive, means, and opportunity to hasten the Eschaton. The "Fundies" may never get another chance that good.

Now consider the untold millions of Cataclysm-awaiting Edgar Cayceites, Nostradamoids, UFO contactees, and devotees of the Eschatonic end-of-time theories of Arguelles and McKenna. Can fifty million Elvis fans be wrong?

The short answer is: "Yes, Virginia, there is no Escape Clause."

The Apocalypse reneged on its promise at the century rollover in the year 1000 AD. Prior to people had sold their possessions, and given up on the world, to fast and do penance as the hour approached. However, the only result was indirect: The economy and productivity of Europe was severely stifled. Work on just about every level of society (in Europe) slowed to a crawl from roughly 950 AD to 1050 AD. When it finally became evident that Judgment Day and God's Kingdom weren't coming, work began again on cathedrals, books were again copied and illuminated, and a search for the reason why began in earnest. The crusading excursions and armies sent to the East may have had this apocalyptic failure in mind. The biggest clue was the Moslem domination of Jerusalem and the Holy Land. Perhaps the Messiah could not fulfill His obligation without His pre-ordained property. Or so the thinking went. Also there was a fear among theologians that perhaps their dates and predictions were wrong because of some yet undiscovered information or artifacts. The search for such clues, and Relics, and the removal of the infidels, were all involved in the creation of the Order of the Knights of the Temple.

For this second millennium time around, one key prerequisite has been met: since 1947 the Jews have returned to the Holy Land. But for the scenario to be completed, a Temple to YHVH must be erected again on the temple mount where now stands the Dome of the Rock Mosque. Certain radical Zionists in Israel are completely ready for the long awaited temple, having all the fittings-including equipment for Old Testament style animal sacrifice-ready and waiting just in case an earthquake or bomb should happen to make the Real Estate available.

Take a look through your English language Bible. You won't find the word "Apocalypse" at all. The original Greek New Testament titles John's Revelation the *Apokalupsis*. People tend to think that "Apocalypse" means "destruction" but in fact it is a Greek word that simply means "revelation." *Apo* means "reversal," and *kaluptein*, "to cover." Thus *Apokalupsis* really means "taking off the covers." The phrase "apocalypse now" has became a cliché associated with chaotic horror, as in the Vietnam War, but it's really something more appropriate to say as you get ready for bed!

Because John's Revelation was placed as the last book of the combined Bible, the Apocalypse became associated with the End. The language of Revelation, with its graphic metaphors for the end of the world, cemented this association of Apocalypse with finality. The New Testament, as a piece of literature, ends with the final war, resurrection, and the New Jerusalem. It does finish on an optimistic note, but only in the context of the prerequisite total annihilation of sinful mankind.

The Hebrew Bible set the mold for the story in John in its final chapter, Malachi 4,

> The day comes, burning like a furnace: all the arrogant and all the evil-doers will be stubble, and that day when it comes will set them ablaze, leaving them neither root nor branch, says the Lord of Hosts. But for you who fear my name, the sun of righteousness will rise with healing in its wings, and you will break loose like calves released from the stall. On the day I take action you will tread down the wicked, for they will be as ashes under the soles of your feet, says the Lord of Hosts...

This one paragraph, that encourages people to be righteous by fearing God, tells them that on the day to come they will enjoy the privilege of treading through the ashes of their enemies. The influence of these final chapters on humanity has been devastating.

It's too bad the Apocryphal Books were excised from the standard Bible because the word *apocryphal* means "hidden away:' If you have a Bible with the "official" Apocrypha, take a look at its ending, The Second Book of Maccabees, Chapter 15, Verses 38 and 39. Your mind is about to be blown.

Think of how Western Civilization might have developed throughout the past two thousand years if these poetic, and enlightened lines had been the final and Ultimate message to humanity,

> At this point I shall bring my work to an end. If it is found to be well written and aptly composed, that is what I myself aimed at; if superficial and mediocre, it was the best I could do. For, just as disagreeable to drink wine by itself or water by itself, whereas the mixing of the two produces a pleasant and delightful taste, so too variety of style in a literary work charms the ear of the reader. Let this, then be my final word. (2 Maccabees 15: 38-39)

Unfortunately, this is the least known Bible passage, one that shows rare humanity, humility, humor, and acknowledges that the writer is a person, a regular human. Bible Fundamentalists who don't use the Apocrypha, point instead to the books of Daniel, Ezekiel and others for detailed catastrophic and messianic prophecies. There is not enough space here or anywhere to refute in detail every horrifying prediction in the Bible.

Sober scholarship has found specific contexts for the supposed prophecies of the Bible. Remember, friends, even though you may have heard that the Bible is the word of God, it wasn't written by God. It was written by hundreds of different people throughout a period of six to twelve hundred years. The original pieces were unrelated historical annals, government propaganda pieces, adaptations of older myths, and individual poetic or prophetic inspirations. It was edited, purged, shuffled, expanded, expunged, and rewritten by hundreds of additional people.

What we have today looks like a unified text, but only because it is all in the same typeface.

Objective Biblical scholarship has been able to de-edit parts of the Bible, by style and vocabulary, back to their original component parts. The "Book of J" and "Book of Q;" modern reconstructions of just two of the original texts buried in the Old and New Testaments, are amazingly non-Apocalyptic.

Many of the so-called prophetic sections of the Bible are pieces that were originally written as a topical social commentary, but "back dated" to show that the present circumstance had been predicted. An analogous situation would be to create a forged diary of Elvis Presley, back-dated to 1972, in which in a Seconal trance, he accurately "predicts" world events of the 1980s-90s. Nowadays even a few people would believe such a ruse. But people were less critical in the past, and the practice of inventing history and prophecy to justify the present was a ancient ruse.

While certain portions of the Bible contain semi-accurate historical information, the book as a whole is a quilt of fiction. Even the most farfetched modern fiction has some elements of truth. But how can such a pastiche, an anthology of fiction, be a reliable source for predicting a universal catastrophe in the year 2000? The answer is: it was not.

Every terrifying Bible-based prophecy–from the Millennialists of a thousand years ago, to the Millerites and Adventists of the last century, to the Jehovah's Witnesses of the twentieth century–has failed to come true. No exegesis or mathematical formula applied to the Bible will provide a more reliable date for Armageddon (which is only mentioned once in the whole Bible, as a place called Har Meggido) because Armageddon is not a preordained truth, it's a literary fantasy. The best selling end-of-the-world prophecy books of Hal Lindsey in the 1970s set the formula for the thousands of similar books which followed. All of these chronologies have failed. Now everyone is focusing on 2012 since the world did not end at the millennium in 2000. I look forward to the day when all these doom predictors will give up and shut up. By rights they should have stopped already.

The best estimate for the birth of "Jesus Christ;' if such a person ever existed at all, based on Herod's census and astronomical recreations of possible "Star of Bethlehem" scenarios, is 6 BC. Two thousand years from 6 BC was 1994. But there's nothing in the Bible anywhere about a two thousand-year span being significant as to the reappearance of the messiah. The two thousand-year thing is a folk fiction, not a scriptural reference. In the Hebrew calendar, the Islamic calendar, and the Chinese calendar, no big "rollover" years are approaching. And more importantly, the world didn't end when the Hebrew or Chinese calendars reached two or four thousand years. Human fate is in our own hands, and is only influenced by the calendar when we make it that way, not because a compulsive day timer-toting God does.

Our "Christian" calendar is divided into BC (Before Christ) and AD (Anno Domini, meaning "in the year of our Lord"). This BC/AD system wasn't even imposed until about 800 AD. Prior to this, there was no universally accepted dating system. The BC/AD system in use, if corrected by our best historical reasoning for the time coincidental with the alleged birth of Jesus, needs to be put back six years. In other words, the social consensus of what era we live in is another arbitrary fiction; we are just too stupid and superstitious to accept it.

Yearning for the Eschaton goes back to Gnosticism. The original Gnostics believed the world we see is so skewed because it was a botched job from the beginning. They taught that the true God is transcendental, but approachable through direct experience by withdrawal from the temptations of the wicked world. Some Gnostics interpreted the Bible to indicate that YHVH is the villain of the piece, the alien god keeping humanity down, and that Lucifer, the bringer of light, is the courageous angel that promises people a way out. If that sounds farfetched or Satanic, one Gnostic idea has filtered down to us today: the idea of the original "flaw"–that this visible world is hopelessly mal-designed and needs to be destroyed to make room for a new one. But just because this notion sounds romantic doesn't make it true. The world is flawed because of humanity's fear of death and loss. Fear inspires irrational violence; scarcity inspires competition and war. But the original Gnostics weren't complaining about the weather. They were complaining about the power of the state, and political and economic oppression. Powerless in the face of brutal totalitarianism, the Gnostics extrapolated that if their situation was eternally hopeless, it was probably some God's will. But their own inner ecstatic experiences, brought on by starvation and perhaps drugs, introduced them to an alternate Inner God, diametrically opposite to the dangerous "God of this World." Given their situation, it's hard to fault their reasoning. Today we know that political oppression is not divinely ordained. But what has filtered down from the Gnostics is their suspicion that the world can't be fixed and isn't worth fixing. And what has been lost is their sense that true divinity is to be achieved through inner work, rather than something outside to be feared and obeyed.

Modem "Apocalyptics" have promulgated this unhealthy message: no future is worth working towards, nothing can be improved, the only solution to our planet's myriad problems is the Second Coming. This kind of thinking is some very dangerous stuff.

Fortunately, Apocalyptic thinking is not universal. Among Christian churches, the Catholics stand out as being at the forefront of down playing prophecy and Bible interpretation.

The Holy Roman Catholic Church, to its core, believes it is the New Jerusalem, and that judgment is ongoing on a case-by-case basis.

The popes never encouraged reading or studying the Bible. It was the technology of the printing press that incited the Reformation, by allowing the Church to print so many indulgences for sale that they began to lose credibility. Likewise, people had access to printed Bibles for the first time, and even a cursory reading proved to the numerous Reformers that the Holy Church was wrong. Nevertheless, the Roman Catholic establishment has survived to the second Millennium of its own Calendar, and it has no intention of being supplanted by a new Messiah that will destroy the old established order.

So the R. C. Church instead builds for the future, with Pope T-shirts, Pope coffee mugs and Pope soap-on-a-rope. Though they will never admit it, Catholics see each Pope as the living Messiah, an "Anointed One" linked to God. When the current megastar Pope dies, his successor will instantly gain the entire fan club, as well as the messianic responsibility. This hugely successful public relations campaign explains why the Catholics are not particularly interested in Apocalypse scenarios.

Jews do await a messiah, but not the end of the world. Orthodox Jewish thinking about the future is generally optimistic. The Jewish resurgence that followed their near-elimination in the Nazi Holocaust is considered by many to be a kind of post-Apocalypse. (Remember that the Apocalypse is a Christian folk myth.) The chosen people of the Torah have returned to the promised land. All that remains is for the Messiah to establish a new Kingdom. When Rebbe Menachem Mendel Schneerson died in 1994 and did not resurrect his followers were utterly stunned. Another ultra orthodox Hassidic group, the Satmar, doesn't even recognize the current political Israeli Nation, and proclaims that the Bible is clear that only the Messiah can establish the post-Diaspora Kingdom.

Because of the establishment of the Jewish State of Israel, Messianic scenarios are possible, although He will presumably have to overthrow the existing government. Jews do not, however, predict doom for non-Jews. Gentiles are considered irrelevant, and immune to God's alleged punishments and rewards to come. To the Orthodox, the only doomed people are liberal Jews and atheist Jews.

The people of Asia have myriad myths describing cycles of creation and destruction but do not eagerly await a Judgment Day the way Evangelicals do. The future Buddha, Maitreya, comes with joy and healing, not destruction. Hindu calendars place us deep in the Kali Yuga, the Dark Age of Ignorance which will last another hundred thousand years or so, to be followed by a Golden Age.

In the Islamic reckoning of time, Year Zero coincides with what we call 622 AD This was the year of Mohammed's Hejira from Mecca, ten years before his death. Moslem civilization is now in its fourteenth century and has utterly no fear about the anticipated Christian Apocalypse. Islam sees itself as the fulfillment of the entire Judea-Christian tradition and concludes that Mohammed was himself the awaited Messiah for all humanity. Case closed. However, certain sects within Islam do have apocalyptic yearnings and await the Imam Madhi, a world savior.

The Mayan Calendar is an incredible piece of scientific/ mythological machinery getting a lot of attention lately. The calendar is based on circular repetitive cycles of time. One grand cycle has been calculated to conclude in the vulgar year 2012. But the idea that this calendar "runs out" in 2012 is preposterous. Circular calendars don't stop, or "finish:' As with the uneventful daily routine of our ordinary wall clocks, the Universe doesn't get "translated" or "magically reconstituted" any more at 12:01 A.M. than at any other moment of the day.

Armageddon Scenarioists point to an Astrological conjunction of May 2000, that they believe Nostradamus referred to. There is an interesting solar system geometry at that time, but it is a cyclical reoccurrence that has never exterminated mankind on previous occasions.

The Earth is billions of years old. Modern humans have been walking this earth for at least a million years. We, as a species, have survived ice ages, volcanoes, comets, earthquakes, wars, diseases, religions and the modern corporate state. Looked at from the long perspective, it is highly unlikely that anything is going to wipe out Humanity down to the last man, woman, and child, and then judge and process their souls.

There are other reasons to be cheerful, at least as far as the alleged Apocalypse is concerned. Investors, banks, funds, foundations and corporate CEO's may be shortsighted and greedy, but they are not operating as if the end of time is imminent. The big multi-national corporate giants have ten- and twenty-year projection plans of where they want their businesses to grow, and what laws and governments are going to have to be "brought on board;' to help make their plans develop profitably and on schedule. To a business planner, the Armageddon Prospectus just doesn't have an attractive Bottom Line.

The danger of Apocalyptic thinking is that abstract fear is transformed into a delusional paranoia. Anticipating Armageddon leads to shoddy work, laziness, poor planning, and avoidance of living in general. There is no incentive in fixing or improving life on earth because what's the use if it's all going to fry in five years?

The dynamism, or bipolarity, of history is unstoppable. There is always an unknown and unpredicted factor. And Humans always rise up against entrenched oppression. Every Regime ever, has failed eventually. The only possible way to end history would be to get each and every human addicted to Prozac. But even then, there would eventually be a strange explosion at the Prozac factory, or a mutation would develop blocking serotonin modifiers. History is not a train on a straight track. It's more like the comingling DNA helixes of spiral pasta. A short term overwhelming victory and domination by one side will only result in an exaggerated reaction from the oppressed.

My own prediction for the future is this: all Bible-based prophecy will continue to fail. Studying the train schedule for a line that no longer exists is useless. Apocalyptics themselves are the only real threat humanity faces. They don't care about pollution, or the need for infrastructure, and they are much more likely to push the button if it comes to it.

The future belongs to the futurists. Rapturous Christians and other Eschatonians don't like to think about the future because they sense they have no place in a post-religious, post "moral" world. They conceive a dream world future for true believers only that mirrors a mythical Eden from the deepest fictional past.

Futurists see the best hope for humanity in the new frontier of Space. Earthbound greed, political expediency, and Authoritarianism are not likely to go away, on an over crowded Planet Earth. These traits are evolutionary survival instincts for closed systems. Elbow room leads to optimism and progressive experimentation. This is why pioneers and counter-culturists have always gone together. And until we can open up new territory, or find a way to stabilize population growth, Apocalyptic Fantasy will be rampant.

The End
BUT NOT
THE END!

Angels, Devils, Spiritual Rebels
Wayne Saalman

[NOTE: This is the chapter 27 from Wayne Saalman's book The Dream Illuminati: A Global Revolution Takes Flight *(New Falcon Publications). The book aims to challenge readers to investigate their belief systems in order to re-evaluate, and ultimately expand, their world view. The author dedicated the New Millennium Edition of his novel to the memory of Dr. Christopher S. Hyatt.]*

On the third day after the massacres in New York and San Francisco, and the bombings in Chicago and Atlanta, it was time to bury the dead.

In New York, there was grieving of a magnitude not seen for years. For thirteen Vimanians had literally fallen from the sky and the funeral was massive, so huge in fact, that a four block radius had to be cordoned off and closed to all traffic in that vicinity.

As a mark of solidarity, the cathedrals in Chicago and Atlanta also held ceremonies within their naves at the same time, and this despite the gaping holes in the sides of their buildings.

In San Francisco, the lone police officer who had been slain was buried in a private ceremony, while in Vimana Cathedral, there were six to be eulogized. The ceremony, now in progress, was also of a magnitude that had not been seen in the city in years. It was full of weeping and joy, as love and condolences went out to the families... And each and all who spoke decried the senselessness of the killings.

Outside the cathedral in the four cities, thousands lined the streets, inevitably some for and some against the Order, but most of the voices were muted now out of respect for the dead and only the national and international media coverage proved to be maddening for everyone involved.

Indeed, story after story was being told, and eulogy after eulogy delivered. The surprise guest in San Francisco was the Reverend Donovan Reaves who strolled humbly into the great nave beside his niece, Heather, and he was pushing Shane Ridley in a chair. His own comment to the clamoring media: "God Almighty has commanded, "Thou shalt not kill." Yet, some of our own have done just that and it is never right. I am here in San Francisco, therefore, out of respect for the dead and to honor the Word of God. Let us heed that Word. Let us all resolve to live together in peace for the sake of the world. Amen."

As the eyes of the world looked on, Kelby rose at last to speak, to deliver the final homily, and to put the tragedy to rest. But Kelby knew that this words would have a limited impact. Those who did not want to hear, would not hear, though his voice would be amplified and carried live across the entire planet. On this day there would be no missing his voice. But not everyone with ears to hear would hear it.

Nevertheless, certain issues needed to be addressed and Kelby intended to do just that.

"Ladies and gentlemen, I speak to you today from the heart," he began, "sad for the loss of life, but hopeful too that greater understanding will prevent further bloodshed in the future and that this tragic occasion will serve to awaken all of us to the preciousness of life and the sanctity of it. There is no point in my setting up an 'us' and 'them' scenario here and arguing that 'we' are better or more right than 'them' and calling for vengeance against the perpetrators of these crimes. Of course certain individuals have conspired to harm us and *have* harmed us. They have done *far more* than simply harm us, they have murdered our own. But should we condemn the individuals alone or the groups to which they belong? Tyler Evans was a Christian and the three gunmen in New York were allegedly, 'Agents of Babylon'. Is traditional Christianity the enemy then? And the agents of Babylon? And are these 'agents', as some say, the Illuminati in disguise? Are they part of a secret Brotherhood? Could they be an extremist faction of the Freemasons as some insist? Or is it the Vatican that colludes with the Brotherhood? Or the Freemason *and* the Catholic Church? In other words, both Protestants and Catholics?! Who are the enemies of the Order of Vimana?

"Some, many, have been editorializing in the last twenty four hours that the Brotherhood is actually *pro*-Vimana and that they perpetrated the whole sniper incident in New York in an effort to gain public sympathy for Vimana. They did this, according to this line of reasoning, so that the dominant social trend in America, and indeed the whole planet, will now move another step closer to a New World Order and that New World Order will effectively supplant traditional Christianity and consolidate power even more-so for the secular government. For this religion they say has proven to be one that has generated conflict. So to have Judaism and the Islamic faith. The proof of that is not just in the Middle East, but all over the planet these days. But nationalism too has caused conflict. Not merely regional conflicts, but world wars. Nevertheless, many of these same writers and pundits on television have noted that such conflicts have actually *served* the world economy and the Powers That Be up to now. It has funneled wealth beyond belief into the hands of these powers.

"Of course, these are different times and different times can call for a change of strategy, a fresh approach. Some say there *should be* a World Government at last. For the world is now very much operating with a global economy. And perhaps it is time for humanity to see the end of entrenched nationalism and religious sectarianism, because our oil resources, which have driven the engine of the global economy for so long now, are dwindling. The planet is polluted now certainly because of our overuse of fossil fuels and the very survival of the earth is at stake finally. The Vimana is obviously the vehicle of the future, they argue. It doesn't pollute and it uses very little fuel of a type which is quite abundant. And once it is licensed for general use by the public, which should be quite soon, these flying machines will be sold to the public and the production of these units will generate jobs, an there will be *serious funds* generated for the world markets and that will greatly enhance the global economy.

"It's a new day, these voices say, and the Powers That Be know that and they are acting on it. They want to move the world in a certain direction and, to do that, certain things must happen and happen fast. We are indeed in a world crisis. No one can doubt that. The fact of it is all around us.

"Many, of course, will say that such talk is nonsense. That the Babylon thing is a cover story for Christian or Islamic terrorists and so on. They will say that it's a menacing and complex world that we live in now and only time and patient investigations by the FBI, by state and local police, will solve this mysterious crime. But how do we answer it all today? How do we make *sense* of it all as we gather here together at this very moment?

"I don't pretend to have all of the answers. But I do have my own insights and I feel that I must speak out today as best I can. I think that we are living in a time of great change and great revelation. A time of great awakening. And though many of the sages in the past have known it and have been telling us this for centuries and millenniums, those who are awakening now are finally fully realizing something very important: that we live in a world of duality, that everything in this world, in fact, is *predicated* on duality and that duality is at the very root of all of our problems.

"What is duality? It is matter and spirit, it is light and dark, protons and electrons, positive and negative energies, subject and object, self and other, you and me... It is good and evil too. From the very inception of life as we know it, dualism is inherent. There is no ignoring it or escaping it. Once this universe was created, absolutely everything within it was subject to dualism. On this science and religion totally agree.

"The point is: there are indeed positive forces in this world and negative forces. They are within each of us and in everyone on the planet. They are in everything that lives on the earth. And we might call these positive and negative forces, Christly forces and Luciferian forces. The Hindus would say they are emanations of Vishnu, the creator, and Shiva, the destroyer. Buddhists would see these forces as impersonal *karmic* forces. They would say that there are no *beings,* or no God, generating these forces, but simply life itself creating them or the universe itself creating them. They would say that we ourselves *are* those forces, and that what we *think, say and do* quite simply comes back to us.

"But labels are just that: labels. We mustn't be fooled by words. Words are a human creation. There is nothing *absolute* about language.

"Still, we *do* think of language as absolute and millions of people down through the centuries have, over and again, fought and killed each other over words and labels. But this is a grave error and always was. The Judeo-Christian-Islamic traditions have been some of the most combative traditions in the world because of words and labels, and especially because of the insistence by so many within these particular traditions that their Holy Books are the absolute, *literal* Word of Yahweh or Allah.

"But is that in fact true? Leaving Islam aside for the moment, let me just give a few examples from the Judeo-Christian Bible that indicates contradiction, the most obvious being God's commandment that 'Thou shall not kill' and then doing that over and over again, smiting entire cities in some cases. If this isn't contradictory, then what is? And if there *is* only one Son of God as Christians insist, then why does the first book of their Bible, Genesis, in Chapter 6 say, 'And it came to pass, when men began to multiply on the face of the earth, and daughters were born unto them, that the Sons of God saw the daughters of men and they were fair; and took them wives all of which they chose.' What does this statement mean if not what it claims to mean? And in the original Greek, the Bible speaks of God as the *Elohim* which is actually a plural form that refers not simply to a monotheistic Deity, but to the *gods*.

"When we examine the four gospels too, Matthew, Mark, Luke and John, we find that the stories there don't always tally. For example, after the crucifixion, once Jesus had been laid to rest in the stone sepulcher, Saint Matthew says that an angel descended from heaven and rolled back the stone on the third day and sat upon it, that the risen Jesus had left the tomb. In Saint Mark the account states that a young man in a white garment was within the empty tomb when the first persons arrived to look in on the body. In Saint Luke, there are *two* men in shining garments and in Saint John *two angels* dressed all in white.

"So if the Bible is literally true, why do we have these discrepancies? And why do we have the prophet Isaiah talking about dragons in Chapter 13, Verse 22, and about fiery flying serpent in Chapter 30, Verse 6 if dragons and flying serpents are unreal? Isaiah speaks of dragons again in Chapter 34, Verse 13, as well as about satyrs in Verse 14 of that same chapter. If these creatures never existed, what is Isaiah talking about? And who are the *Nefilim* that are alluded to in Genesis? Most early translators simply called them giants. Chapter 6, Verse 6, states that, 'There were giants in the earth in those days; and also after that, when the Sons of God came in unto the daughters of men, and they bare children to them, the same became mighty men which were of old, men of renown.' So if there were indeed giants on the earth in those days, then where are the bones? Where is the proof? Or could these Nefilim be some other group? There is at least one highly regarded translator of ancient languages who says that this term really means, 'Those Who Descended' or 'Those Who Fell From the Heavens'. And if these beings are indeed the Sons of God and they did indeed interbreed with the daughters of men, we have a very interesting lineage springing up at this juncture in history. Some say that these very beings are the ones we now refer to as the Illuminati and that their symbol is the serpent, and also the dragon, and that they are with us still, and that they yet orchestrate events behind the scenes in this world of ours. Perhaps, then, they have even orchestrated these very events that have brought us here *today*...

"I will let you think on that... But I will point out one further facet to consider in this matter. The biblical story of the Garden of Eden says that God told Adam and Eve not to touch the fruit of a certain tree. And it states in Genesis, in Chapter 2, Verse 9, that, '...out of the ground made the Lord God to grow every tree that is pleasant to the sight, and good for food; the tree of life also in the midst of the garden, and the tree of knowledge of good and evil.' And then in Chapter 3, Verse 5, the 'Serpent' tells Eve that she should eat of the tree, 'For God doth know that in the day ye eat there-of, then your eyes shall be opened, and ye shall be as gods, knowing good and evil.' In the New Testament too, in John 10:34, Jesus cries out, echoing this idea, 'Is it not written in your law, I said, Ye are gods?"

"Can we really be as gods by eating of the tree of life and knowing good and evil? Can we be as gods if we but see into our essential nature, a nature predicated on dualism? Can we all be like the Gnostics of old, the first real Christians, whose very name means 'Knowers'? Can we too be like the initiates in the Pagan Mysteries who understood that knowledge of God was only possible if one had a direct spiritual epiphany or experience of God. Have you heard that in knowing yourself, you know God?"

"In the book of Isaiah in the Bible, Chapter 45, Verses 6 and 7, it states quite explicitly, 'I am the Lord and there is none else. I form the light, and create darkness: I make peace and create evil: I the Lord do all these things.'

"This is an amazing statement really. It is an *extraordinary admission*, in fact, and it is time that we all face the music together, that we face reality itself, and understand that by our very nature we are both peace loving at times and violent at times. We do good some days, but other days we can and do make terrible mistakes, and say things that we don't really mean, and we hurt our loved ones or our neighbor. Every human being acts impulsively at times, and quite selfishly too. We don't put others first sometimes and that is where we fall down. But if we truly understand what that means, that we are ever inherently dualistic beings, then we will certainly be more forgiving of ourselves and our fellow humans too. For everybody errs and loses their head sometimes. Mistakes are made.

"Originally, the word 'sin' was a term used in archery where a bows man misses the mark. That is sin exactly, I say. It is a missing of the mark, plain and simple. God surely understands that. It happens and it is forgivable because mortal beings err at times and do that. But if a person learns from a mistake, he or she grows.

Of course, if one *intends* to cause hurt or harm, that is evil. That is being a fool. For we do reap what we sow and such evil will certainly come back on us, and we will pay a great price. By *causing* others to suffer in this world, we cause *ourselves* to suffer.

"But we must show compassion to one and all, even the fools among us, because we are all alike in essence. And it doesn't really matter if we are natives of this earth or if we came here in ancient times from the heavens, from some other planet entirely. We are all members of God's family. Or to put it another way, we are all at one with what the Greeks called the *Pneuma*, the Spirit, and what the ancient Chinese called the *Tao*, the Hindus the *Akasha*, the Buddhists the *Buddha Mind*, and what scientists today call the Zero Point Field, that unnamable Original Essence or Force that gives rise to the quantum universe itself in all of its cosmic grandeur and diversity.

"But no matter how we look at these matters, nor what we decide about them, it is time for the ruling elite to begin treating every soul on this planet as equals finally and to begin showing us more mercy and to be more concerned with the plight of the poor, and with those who do not even have enough food or clean water for themselves. Conversely, it is also time for those who feel frustrated and powerless, and bitter towards those who rule and possess ungodly riches, to understand that such beings or people arrived at their position in life by sowing *positive* karmic seeds sometime in the past, seeds that blossomed in such a way that these beings now have what they have today. We all evolve at our own pace and in our own way. And in lifetime after lifetime, as souls reincarnate, they sometimes assume the role of the rich and sometimes the role of the poor. The Christian Gnostics believed this back in their day as much as the Hindus and the Buddhists do today. But once the concept of reincarnation was put into the hands of the ruling Roman emperors, Constantine and those after him, the concept was made a heresy. For it interfered with their own power. So they came up with an alternative concept. They told the people that they lived only *once* and that when they died they went either to heaven or hell for all of eternity. And only the priests could intermediate with God for them. And only the Church could save their souls from eternal damnation. But this concept is wrong. It is dead wrong. And it causes, and has caused, more suffering on this earth perhaps than any other concept ever devised.

"In truth, a soul lives on, over and over, projecting itself into various planes where certain causes and conditions prevail. But this life, or any other, is ultimately just another round on the Great Wheel of Life. And every lifetime is for learning spiritual lessons and for soul growth. And if we do happen to be one of the ruling elite in this lifetime, we would do well to remember those wise words from both Matthew and Mark in the Bible, 'For what shall it profit a man if he shall gain the whole world and lose his own soul?'

"I don't believe that Jesus exists the way that traditional Christianity says he exists, but I do believe that the *teachings of Jesus* are valid and true. I also believe that if anyone finds it spiritually uplifting and inspiring to believe in a personal Jesus, a Jesus who is the one and only Savior of Humankind, and if that article of faith gives hope and makes that person a better person, then fine. But don't be intolerant of those who see things otherwise.

I also don't believe that Satan exists the way that traditional religions in the West would have it. But there are

Luciferian forces, forces that give rise to greed, to envy, selfishness, jealousy, hatred, vengeance and so on. These forces are indeed real, but they are quite simply lower forces that automatically arise in a dualistic world and serve to offer a contrast to the good. For without contrast, nothing can be understood nor have any meaning for us.

"And if you really find it difficult and hard to understand what the Order of Vimana is all about, I would say open up your Bible and look up some of the passages that I have quoted here today. Turn to Joel in the Old Testament and note where it says, 'Your sons and your daughters shall prophesy, and your old men shall dream dreams, your young men shall see visions.' Members of the Order do exactly that: dream dreams and then become visionaries. For that is precisely how the world evolves and becomes a better place, a place where people really *can* love their enemies, as Christ had hoped. A place where people are *pure in heart* and cease acting out of ulterior motives. Where the peacemakers really are blessed and called the children of God. Where people really do understand that we reap what we sow and that one should indeed love they neighbor as thyself.

" Please understand that if Jesus really did exist historically, then there is a certain fact about him that cannot be ignored. And it is this: Jesus was a rebel in his day! He set out to purposely overturn the old order and to break with many of the laws and customs of the Jewish culture. So maybe being spiritual rebel is not such a bad thing after all and maybe it is by rebellion that cultures break into new territory. The Protestant revolution is certainly another example of rebellion and the scale of that was enormous. So keep these points in mind when you go judging the actions of those of us involved with the Vimana movement. For we are not out to destroy the older order, but to enrich it and thereby create a fresh order, a twenty-first century order, but one founded on freedom and liberty for all, and not the dreaded 'New World Order' that is talked about by conspiracy theorists, an order that is as oppressive as ever, and as cold and calculating as ever, which many believe of the secret elite known as the Illuminati. What Vimanians want is a new order that rings as true in its metaphysics as in its science, an order that is compassionate and caring. We only ask that you give us a chance to prove that we can achieve that.

"To begin then, I will tell you that we Vimanians won't seek vengeance on those among you who have taken a certain twisted delight in the suffering that have been inflicted upon us. We know better. For we shall be as gods, knowing good and evil...We understand that karma isn't what happens to you, but *what you make happen*.

"And we know something else too... Christ is risen. The Redemption has come and the Ascension too. To fly, is to know that and to be at one with the angels.

"I stand before you grieving today, and emotionally exhausted but I am determined, more than ever, to help turn this world around and to put it on the right path. I am determined to do this regardless of what any religious extremists may throw at me or what any Powers That Be may do. And if the truth is to set us free, then we must *freely face the truth* and do what we know in our heart of hearts to be best.

There is a new heaven and a new earth before us now, and we must wipe away the tears from each other's eyes and see death for what it is, *transformation*. Death is not the opposite of life, but quite simply a process within it. The opposite of life is nothingness. But nothingness can never be. For life itself is the proof of that.

"All evolution within the *Whole* relies on the transformation of one thing into its opposite. So everything must return at last. Even me and even you. In some form. In some fresh form.

"With the deepest of perceptions, when one at last learns to identify with the eternal soul rather than with the mortal body, then one may finally understand that death is not the horror it is believed to be. Death is simply a part of the natural order in a world founded on causes and conditions. As the great poet, Walt Whitman, once wrote in his poem *Song of Myself*,

> What do you think has become of the young and the old men (who have died)?
> And what do you think has become of the women and children?
> They are alive and well somewhere.
> The smallest sprout shows there is really no death...
> All goes onward and outward, nothing collapses,
> And to die is different from what any one supposed, and luckier.
> Has any one supposed it lucky to be born?
> I hasten to inform him or her it is just as lucky to die, and I know it.
> I pass death with the dying and birth with the new-washed babe, and am not contained between my hat and boots...
> I am not an earth or adjunct of the earth,
> I am the mate and companion of people, all just as immortal and fathomless as myself,
> (They do not know how immortal, but I know.)

"I know it too," Kelby said decisively. "And what is it, only suffering and death, that impels a human to even consider the spiritual side of life? It is death and suffering that causes us to have empathy and compassion, and to even *think about* anything beyond this material world.

"Maybe you do not know how immortal you are, but I know." He choked slightly on these words as they came forth from him now, but only because he was thinking of his own father, for he had read these very words of Whitman's a this father's funeral and they never failed to summon tremendous emotion.

But Kelby pressed on, paraphrasing the Bible now. "In that day, when such a perception fills us, there will be no more death, neither sorrow, nor crying, neither shall there be any more pain: for the former things are passed away, we will say. And joy and eternal bliss will be ours forever.

"Life is about one thing," he said, "spiritual enrichment. It is about spiritual enrichment and virtually all of our pleasures and pains contribute to that enrichment. So love life as it is and live it with exuberance an a pure heart. It is yours because you are lie. And I have had my say now and I can do little else only wish you peace forever and ever. Amen."

Contributing Authors

S. Jason Black was a professional writer, illustrator, fine artist and a lifelong student and practitioner of Magic and Tantra. He worked as a professional psychic, and was much sought after for his accuracy.

Robert Brazil, a brilliant researcher, astrologer, and magician, passed away in 2010. A key early member of TAHUTI Lodge in New York City, he was knowledgeable and sophisticated, with a profoundly ironic sense of humor and an eclectic erudition. He pursued his fascination with William Shakespeare and was actively engaged with the historical controversy of the writer's identity.

David Cherubim was a musician, magician, and author. He was the head of the Thelemic Order of the Golden Dawn and author of *Diary of the Antichrist* and an excellent editor for New Falcon Publications.

Chic Cicero has authored books on subjects including the Golden Dawn, tarot, and ceremonial magic with his wife, S. Tabatha Cicero. Having established a Golden Dawn temple in 1977, Chic was one of the key people who helped his friend Israel Regardie to resurrect a legitimate, initiatory branch of the Hermetic Order of the Golden Dawn in the United States in the early 1980s.

S. Tabatha Cicero is a member of several Co-Masonic, Martinist, and Rosicrucian organizations. She met her husband and co-author Chic Cicero in the early 1980s and the Golden Dawn system of magic has been her primary spiritual focus ever since.

Peter Conte carries forth the torch of the Magickal Childe Bookstore in New York City where he read Tarot cards for many years. Peter embodies the shop's motto, "Hard Core, New Age." He is currently writing a book on the Tarot which promises to be very thorough.

Lon Milo DuQuette is a noted Tantric authority who has written and taught extensively in the areas of Mysticism, Freemasonry, Tarot, Qabalah, ceremonial magic, Enochian magic, spirit evocation, and the Goetia. He is the co-author with Christopher S. Hyatt of several New Falcon Publication titles.

Eric Gullichsen has been involved with computers and programming for more than four decades. He has written in the areas of hypertext, logic programming languages, and digital logic.

Steven Heller, Ph.D. was widely in demand as a clinician, lecturer and trainer of the Ericksonian method, which he helped develop, as well as his own method, Unconscious Restructuring. Dr. Heller received his Ph.D. in clinical psychology from California Western University, where his special area of study was hypnosis.

William S. Hyatt, the son of Christopher S. Hyatt, is a writer, an entrepreneur and a critical observer of human behavior in the style of his father.

Richard Kaczynski, Ph.D. is a psychologist specializing in non-mainstream religious beliefs. He has written extensively and lectured internationally on mystical and magical beliefs and practices.

Timothy Leary, Ph.D. was a respected Harvard psychology professor who became a guru for hundreds of thousands of people, espousing the use of the powerful hallucinogen LSD and other mind-altering drugs as a means of brain change. After he was forced out of academia, Leary became associated with many of the great names of the time including Aldous Huxley, Allen Ginsberg, William Burroughs and Charlie Mingus. He died in 1996. Dr. Leary is the author of the New Falcon titles: *What Does WoMan Want?*, *The Intelligence Agents*, *Info-Psychology*, and *Neuropolitique*.

Jeff Mandon has been a student of spiritual development for more than 45 years. Formerly an actor, Jeff has worked in theatre as well as both film and television. During the 1990s Jeff was one of the core cast of the show "In Our Lives," for which he wrote many episodes. His work garnered the Parents Choice Award, the Action for Children's Television award, and a regional Emmy nomination. The essay in this book is culled from his upcoming title, *"CRUMBS... And Other Things I've Followed Home."* Jeff has also worked as a sculptor primarily in the medium of cast bronze.

Shelley Marmor is a freelance journalist for both print and web publications. She has been an ardent student of Christopher Hyatt since her magical studies brought his writings into her life. This was her first major book publishing assignment.

Osho, known also as Bhagwan Shree Rajneesh, was born in India in 1932 and died in 1990. He stands as one of the most famous religious leaders of modern times. He probably hold the record for being thrown out of, or refused entry into, the greatest number of countries in history. He is the author of the New Falcon title *Rebellion, Revolution & Religiousness*. His life and his work should be inspirations to rebels everywhere.

Daniel Pineda is a martial artist, practitioner of the Mystery Traditions, and a devotee of liberty. He holds Black Belts in and teaches various Eastern and Western martial disciplines, as well as Qigong. He lives in south Florida with his wife Julia, with whom he operates Falcon Martial Arts Academy. He is the author of *The Book of Secrets* published by Redwheel Weiser.

Dr. Israel Regardie was an Adept of the Golden Dawn. At an early age, Regardie worked as Aleister Crowley's personal secretary. Regardie was the messenger to the modern world charged with preserving the teachings of Crowley and the Golden Dawn. In addition to his extensive writings, Regardie practiced as a Chiropractor and Therapist. He taught psychiatry at the Los Angeles College of Chiropractic and contributed articles to many psychology magazines.

Wayne Saalman has traveled extensively throughout North America, Europe, Asia, Africa, and Australia in his quest for understanding and insight into the nature and historic origins of human metaphysics. A spiritual syncretist, he personally practices both Gnostic and Buddhist forms of meditation, and draws heavily on the shamanism, magick, yoga, Tantra, Tai Chi, and Chi Kung.

James Wasserman studied and practiced the magical system of Aleister Crowley since the late 1960s. He was a noted author of numerous books on esoteric symbolism, magick, and secret societies, as well as a passionate advocate for the values expressed in the Declaration of Independence, the U.S. Constitution, and the Bill of Rights. The photos he contributed to this book are shown in color in *Secrets of Masonic Washington*.

Dr. Jack S. Willis has graduate degrees in Biochemistry and Psychology and is a Doctor of Chiropractic Medicine. He trained in Reichian Therapy with Dr. Israel Regardie for nine years. A close friend of Dr. Hyatt's, he served as director of the Reichian Therapy Center in Los Angeles, California.

Robert Anton Wilson was the author of numerous books on such wide-ranging subjects as quantum mechanics, UFOs, history, science fiction, sex, mind-altering drugs, mysticism, scientists (pompous and otherwise), secret societies and, especially, human consciousness. They include the best selling New Falcon titles: *Cosmic Trigger Trilogy, Sex, Drugs, & Magick: A Journey Beyond Limits, Prometheus Rising, The New Inquisition, Reality Is What You Can Get Away With, The Walls Came Tumbling Down, Coincidance: A Head Test, Wilhelm Reich in Hell,* and *Quantum Psychology.*

New Falcon Publications
**Publisher of Controversial Books and CDs
Invites You to Visit Our Website:
http://www.newfalcon.com**

At the Falcon website you can:

- Browse the online catalog of all our great titles, including books by Robert Anton Wilson, Christopher S. Hyatt, Israel Regardie, Aleister Crowley, Timothy Leary, Osho, Lon Milo DuQuette and many more
- Find out what's available and what's out of stock
- Get special discounts
- Order our titles through our secure online server
- Find products not available anywhere else including:
  – One of a kind and limited availability products
  – Special packages
  – Special pricing
- And much, much more

Get online today at http://www.newfalcon.com

LUCIFER'S REBELLION